Homeschooling
EASY
COMPANION

by 5-STAR AUTHOR
Lorraine Curry

God's Gardener
www.godsgardener.com

Easy Homeschooling COMPANION

by **5-STAR AUTHOR**
Lorraine Curry

Exhortation
Advice, Persuasion, Admonition, Warning, Guidance, Direction, Counsel, Suggestion, Recommendation, Prescription, Prompting

Encouragement
Cheer, Comfort, Consolation, Hope, Inspiration, Reassurance, Motivation, Assurance, Emboldenment

Ideas
Patterns, Plans, Proposals, Suggestions, Concepts, Principles, Teachings, Theory, Thoughts, Guidelines, Models

The definitions for "Exhortation" and "Encouragement" are adapted from the etext of *Roget's Thesaurus* No. Two, which is derived from the 1911 *Roget's Thesaurus*. (Public Domain) The words for "Ideas" are © 2003 by Merriam-Webster, Inc. from their online resource site: *http://www.m-w.com/cgi-bin/thesaurus*

by **5-STAR AUTHOR**
Lorraine Curry

Copyright © 2004 by Lorraine Curry
ISBN: 0-9709965-1-9
First Edition 2004

All Scripture quotations, unless otherwise specified, are from *King James Version* of the Bible.

Definitions, unless otherwise specified, are derived from *the American Heritage Electronic Dictionary.* © 1993, Houghton, Mifflin Co.

Cover and Illustration: Jennifer Enfinger
Interior Design: *Lorraine Curry*
    Illustrations based on Curry Family photos.
Contributors: *Teresa Jennings Robinson; Jean Hall; Jennifer Robinson; Janet Barber; Priscilla Blanchard; Jessica, Zephi, Ezra and Eli Curry.*

God's Gardener
www.godsgardener.com

Special Thanks To My

Editing Team
Wonderful, Willing, Encouraging and Qualified Homeschoolers

Teresa Jennings Robinson
Blanchard, OK
Mother of three, homeschooling for fourteen years. Legislative and community liaison. Founder of the Oklahoma Home Educators Network.

Trece Wyman
Beaver, WV
Pastor's wife, mother of three daughters. Homeschooling for seventeen years. Double BA in English and Theatre.

Melissa Worcester
Galway NY
Mother of two sons, homeschooling for five years. Former reviewer for Practical Homeschooling *magazine. Web designer and editor.*

Caren Cornell
Maysville GA
Mother of two sons, homeschooling for eight years. Homeschool business owner, web designer and motivational speaker.

Jean Hall
Portland OR
Mother of three daughters, homeschooling for nine years. Technical, fiction and music writer.

Contents

Dingbat Key

✔ Teaching tip or technique

✗ General tip or technique

➻ Notebook activity

☆ Especially important statement

❀ How-to instructions in *Easy Homeschooling Techniques*

☞ Resource or other information in back of this book

✍ Vintage or out of print book

There are many books and resources mentioned within *Easy Home-schooling Companion.* They may be acquired from various sources, such as the companies listed in the resource section in the back of this book, your local Christian bookstore, general bookstore or the public library. You may also go to our site and see our selection of vintage *Exceptional! Books.* While there, take advantage of our FREE resources—copywork selections to print for your children, reviews, articles, authors' biographies and a monthly newsletter.

www.easyhomeschooling.com

The Teacher's Dream

W. H. Venable, ✍ *Poetic Pearls,* 1887

The weary teacher sat alone
    While twilight gathered on;
And not a sound was heard around,
    The boys and girls were gone.

The weary teacher sat alone
    Unnerved and pale was he;
Bowed 'neath a load of care, he spoke
    In sad soliloquy.

"Another round, another round
    Of labor thrown away—
Another chain of toil and pain,
    Dragged through a tedious day.

Of no avail is constant zeal,
    Love's sacrifice is loss,
The hopes of morn, so golden, turn,
    Each evening, into dross.

I squander on a barren field
    My strength, my life, my all;
The seed I sow will never grow,
    They perish where they fall."

He sighed, and low upon his hands,
    His aching brow he prest:
And o'er his frame, ere long there came
    A soothing sense of rest.

And then he lifted up his face,
    And started back aghast—
The room by strange and sudden change
    Assumed proportions vast.

It seemed a Senate-hall, and one
    Addressed a listening throng;
Each burning word all bosoms stirred,
    Applause rose loud and long.

The 'wildered teacher thought he knew
    The speaker's voice and look,
"And for his name," said he, "the same
    Is in my record book."

The stately Senate-hall dissolved—
    A church rose in its place,
Wherein there stood a man of God,
    Dispensing words of grace.

And though he spoke in solemn tone,
    And though his hair was gray,
The teacher's thought was strangely wrought—
    "I whipped that boy to-day."

The church, a phantasm, vanished soon—
    What saw the teacher then?
In classic gloom of alcoved room
    An author plied his pen.

"My idlest lad!" the teacher said,
    Filled with a new surprise—
"Shall I behold his name enrolled
    Among the great and wise?"

The vision of a cottage home,
    The teacher now descried;
A mother's face illumed the place
    Her influence sanctified.

"A miracle! A miracle!"
    This matron well I know,
Was but a wild and careless child,
    Not half an hour ago.

"And when she to her children speaks
    Of duty's golden rule,
Her lips repeat, in accents sweet,
    My words to her at school."

The scene was changed again, and lo,
    The school-house rude and old,
Upon the wall did darkness fall,
    The evening air was cold.

"A dream!" the sleeper, waking, said,
    Then paced along the floor,
And whistling slow and soft and low,
    He locked the school-house door.

And, walking home, his heart was full
    Of peace and trust and love and praise;
And singing slow and soft and low,
    He murmured, "After many days."

Foreword

*L*orraine Curry has provided her readers with a potpourri of scripturally-based homeschooling advice, exhortation and encouragement. Mrs. Curry's style is loose and free-flowing, yet organized. With scriptures, quotes and poetry sprinkled throughout the text, the reader doesn't get bogged down in tedious prose. There are so many nuggets of gold in this book that I advise reading it with a highlighter and also with a notebook and pen in hand. If your philosophy differs in some respect from hers, gently pass over those areas and go on to harvest many wonderful ideas which will enrich your life and your homeschool.

Chapter 1, "Gathering Flowers," is a lovely bouquet of thoughts with an almost stream-of-consciousness feel. When I started reading the book I was surprised by this chapter (expecting, instead, to begin with very practical homeschooling advice). As I read on, I began to get a feel for the author's style, philosophy and thinking, and started my note-taking.

I especially liked (and was convicted by!) Chapter 2, "Pursuing Better Parenting." Rooted in scripture, the exhortations included in this chapter will help parents to examine their priorities, and get back to basics—raising godly children.

"Cultivating Christian Curriculum" (Chapter 3) differs from most chapters and books on curriculum. Mrs. Curry divides curriculum into 3 areas: What is necessary, what is useful, and what is ornamental. What is necessary comprises that which will build the child's character, and that information is found in Scripture alone. Therefore, the Bible must be the foundation of education. That which is useful comprises the 3 R's, as well as less important disciplines such as civics, cultures, languages, history and science. The ornamental is made up of all else, and can easily be mastered after the child has learned to consistently obey God, has become proficient in the basics, and is diligent at study.

Chapter 4, "Drawing from my Diary," is a delightful peek into the Curry's family and homeschool. I wish I could say my own experience was similar!

Chapter 5, "Harvesting from History," takes a look at the philosophy of educators from the time of Milton (17th century) up to John Dewey (19th-20th century). The vignettes provide a wonderful overview of the development of these various philosophies.

Mrs. Curry provides much practical advice in Chapter 6, "Raising the Standard." The primary medium recommended for instruction is recitation, as opposed to rote learning. Recitation—defined as "the rehearsal of a prepared lesson by students before their instructor"—can be used in any area of the curriculum with the benefit that the material is transferred from short-term memory to long-term memory. In addition, using this time-honored method, students will become more reflective, productive, and refined, and more precise in the use of their native language.

"Reaping from Reviews" (Chapter 7) succinctly highlights the main messages of several books. More than reviews, these passages enable the reader to gather, in just a few paragraphs each, the wisdom offered by the various authors.

In Chapter 8 ("Loving Literature"), Mrs. Curry conveys her love for literature as well as advice for using literature-based learning in your own homeschool. Classic literature stimulates the brain (it may take a while for a student whose tastes in reading have been 'dumbed-down' to begin to appreciate the loftier language of the true classics) and most importantly, "elevates the spirit of man, refining thought, character and emotions."

Chapter 9, "Producing Fruit," was my favorite chapter, along with Chapter 2. How we all would like to see the good fruit of the Spirit in our lives and in our homeschools! By examining each of the fruits mentioned in Galatians (love, joy, peace, patience, gentleness, goodness, faith, meekness and temperance), we can work on those qualities which will most change our hearts and those of our children. It seems fitting that Mrs. Curry should end the book with this chapter, since the education we give our children will hopefully, and by God's grace, result in an abundance of spiritual fruit in the lives of our children, in their children, and in the lives of our descendants down to the 1,000th generation!

Mary Lou Posch
Homeschooling mother of five
Wife of Robert Posch, Senior VP of BOOKSPAN

Preface

*L*ong ago the phrases, "on time," "ahead of time" and "behind time" meant nothing.[1] There were neither appointments to keep nor clocks to watch. The day was lived by the sun, moon and stars—the lights God set in the heavens to divide the day from the night. Suppose *you* are living in this unhurried time.

The carriage is well-appointed. The team is well-matched—sleek and elegant. You are attired in your finest. That color always flattered you so! You step up—with help—and settle in. This excursion will take you over miles and methods and counsel from the near and distant past.

It is dark yet, but the horses whinny and toss their manes, eager to depart. The buggy sways as it begins to move slowly out of the drive. Dawn breaks, revealing dozens and dozens of dew-diamonds dancing on the pasture grass. Rosy waters glisten while the buggy begins its uphill climb to our home above Deer Creek.

I have been expecting you.

Stepping down from the carriage, you breathe in the invigorating morning air while breathing out heart-praise to God. From the arbor, we wind our way toward the house through the cottage garden, our senses saturated with colors and fragrances amplified by the warming sun. You have come at the right time—it seems everything is in bloom! We gather some of your favorites, step into the entry and place them in a vase on the piano to await your departure.

Sunlight beams through leaded glass and glimmers on the floral tea service awaiting us in the library. We enter and begin gathering books from the tall bookcases. Soon we are seated and I pour the tea as you peer into my "Learning Diary." We then review old volumes and gather ideas from historical education. After conversing of books and ideas, we turn the last page of the last book.

It is time to meet the schoolmaster. We walk to the schoolhouse near the edge of town and enter the bright white building. As our eyes adjust to the dim interior, we take our places near the blackboard. The meticulous schoolmaster satiates us with thought-provoking teaching. Our hearts and minds are so full, we can hardly keep our thoughts within! We talk of titles we have enjoyed in the past, and of the wisdom of using literature for education.

Soon you will depart, full of sweet memories and new knowledge, yet the best remains as we stop by the orchard, where the Master Gardener teaches us how to grow an abundant harvest of luscious spiritual fruit. This good fruit will result in healthy "seedlings"—children who bring glory to God and honor to their parents.

EasyHomeschooling

My first book, *Easy Homeschooling Techniques,* tells succinctly how to homeschool. I avoided personal anecdotes and excessive verbiage to provide more usable material for the reader. I still refuse to clutter your time and brain with useless or difficult material, but in this book, I do share some softer content, such as the essays in Chapter 1, "Gathering Flowers."

EasyHomeschooling encompasses concepts that are economical and efficient, yet result in well-educated children. Reading is one of these concepts. It has been proven that early and continued reading aloud is the best educational foundation. Consider Marie Curie's "homeschooling."

Every Saturday for years past, M. Sklodovski, his son and three daughters had passed the whole evening together in the pursuit of literature. . . . The old man recited poetry or read aloud, and his children listened to him with rapture: the professor . . . had a remarkable talent for speech. Saturday after Saturday the masterpieces of the past were brought to Manya in this way by a familiar voice. In the old days that voice had told fairy tales, read stories of travel or initiated her into David Copperfield, *which M. Sklodovski transposed into Polish without a hitch as he read from the English text.*[2]

Literature-based learning results in well-educated children. Our daughter, Zephi, tested in the upper tenth percentile of students taking college entrance exams. Zephi took on intensive reading of advanced material during her fifteenth summer. The next school year she focused on advanced math courses, completing both Calculus and Physics. She resolved to graduate at age sixteen.

My prerequisite for providing a ceremony and reception was a speech. She kept hers secret and blessed us with the following on her graduation day. It reveals a fulfillment of the goals for our children's education and also reveals generational faith in Christ—our most important goal.

When I have recovered, Mrs. Curry, from your kind but too generous introduction, I will, I hope, get my mind sufficiently cleared to make a few pertinent remarks. I thank each of you most heartily for making me so inexpressibly happy by your presence on this impressive and, for me, memorable occasion!

I regard the privilege of addressing you today as imposing upon me two obligations: first, that of being brief; second, that of saying such things only as are calculated to merit the attention of ladies and gentlemen whose time is as precious as yours is. For breach of the first obligation, I should be without excuse but the second involves such difficulties that I must rely upon your kind forbearance if I fall short.

Ecclesiastes 9:11 states that "the race is not to the swift, nor the battle to the strong, neither yet bread to the wise, nor yet riches to men of understanding, nor yet favour to men of skill; but time and chance happeneth to them all."

I've been homeschooled in Rockville all of my life, officially starting first grade at age five. One of my earliest memories is of learning to read at the same time as my older sister, Jessica. We were both to graduate this spring, but by a queer twist of fate, she graduated last December. Thus I am a "class of one in 2001."

Most of my education consisted of the basics: reading, writing and arithmetic (my order of preference being reading, arithmetic and writing). I have read, probably, thousands of books in my lifetime; and probably hundreds of those, I've read at least twice. My favorite and most read book is the Bible, King James Version, and I am in the process of reading it for the tenth time. I did not start reading the Bible cover to cover until I was already in high school, but it has always been my favorite book.

Arithmetic has always come fairly easily to me and I have recently completed in one semester, books that were intended for two to four semesters. Because of all the antique books I've read, my writing can be quite good (but writing has never appealed to me very much). Because of a long acquaintance with my favorite animal, much of my writing consists of fictitious cat stories.

Extracurricular activities are many and unusual. I am not your typical athlete and I cannot play any musical instrument well. Mom taught me sewing, crocheting and cooking. I created my first entire meal when I was eight years old! Dad took me fishing and taught me to enjoy cleaning the fish afterwards. I was four years old when I caught my first fish—a twelve-inch carp! I taught myself origami, the Japanese art of paper folding. On my own, I also learned calligraphy and Spencerian penmanship.

How is it possible to graduate high school after never attending "school" a day in my life? How is it possible to read and write and cipher without ever having been to school? How is it possible to receive "homework" from "teachers" when I've never been to school? (The usual place to get homework, I'm told.) How is it possible that I've received high ACT scores when I've never been to school a day in my life? How is it possible that I'm graduating high school at sixteen years of age?

Zephi, 18, recently completed— Summa Cum Laude—her first year at Bible college, majoring in Cross- Cultural Ministries.

Do you think that "homeschool" is the answer? No, it is not. "Surely," you may think, "that is the answer! Nothing else could explain it." Indeed homeschooling is a large part of it. If I'd been in public schools all my life I probably wouldn't have graduated for one or two more years; I probably would have received lower ACT scores and I certainly wouldn't be making this speech! Furthermore, you would have never attended such a unique graduation ceremony.

The answer is found in Jeremiah 32:27. God says, "Behold, I am the Lord, the God of all flesh; is there any-thing too hard for me?" There is nothing too hard for God. If He had so wished, I could have graduated years ago. Nevertheless, He has a plan in everything. He wanted me to be able to say, "I'm a class of one in 2001." He wanted you to be here on my Graduation. For many of you, if I had graduated as little as one year earlier, you would have missed it.

God is in charge and knows where I'm headed. I'm going to keep following Him and keep doing my best. Jesus takes care of the rest. Ecclesiastes 7:8 says, "Better is the end of a thing than the beginning thereof." Better is the end of high school, than the beginning thereof. Much better is

*the end of this speech than the beginning thereof! God bless
you all, and God bless America.*

My Statement of Faith

Zephi's grandmother also graduated at sixteen—from Rockville High
School, next to the gym where we held Zephi's ceremony. This
grandmother—my mother—modeled to me unflinching faith and
optimism during the storms of my childhood. As a young adult, I
met Jesus Christ when someone shared the life-changing Word of
God with me. I began filling myself with the Scriptures and faith
came, as those same Scriptures say it will (Rom. 10:17). I have
learned that God's word is true by "putting it to the test"—by standing on it alone in the past for serious needs, as well as seeing the
Lord provide thereby for all my daily needs and desires. What God
says, I believe. That is my Statement of Faith.

Around the Bend

This book in your hands, when heeded, is a hedge against the
kingdom of darkness as your children are raised for Christ, a light in
the darkness of confusion and despair when daily duties threaten to
overwhelm, and a filter to quiet the clatter of excess curriculum,
activities and requirements. While you gather ideas and information, may you also find encouragement and motivation within its
pages. May *Easy Homeschooling Companion* be a respite from
today's lifestyles that will carry beyond its reading.

We are about to begin our excursion. We will disregard any ruts
in the road or thorns in the garden. The panoramic beauty of God's
plan will far overshadow such minor discomforts.

1

Gathering Flowers

A Bouquet of Essays

Consider the lilies of the field, how they grow; they toil not, neither do they spin: and yet I say unto you, that even Solomon in all his glory was not arrayed like one of these (Matt. 6:28, 29).

The Sorensen family lived in our house from 1917 to 1961. The day lilies that Mrs. Sorensen planted have multiplied for eighty-five years and present a glorious orange display when in bloom.[1] However, the prettiest gardens and arrangements exhibit variety. This chapter is like that. Just watch out for the thorns! Rose vines prick, yet roses in full bloom are beautiful. The thorns cannot prevent the force of blooming. Likewise the Maker's perfect plan unfolds in our lives.

- TV content, psychiatry and other concerns prick like thorns, but knowledge equips for victory and directs us into the right paths. (Is. 30:21)

- Seeing my mother confined for years was excruciating. Then in the midst of her darkest night, eternal springtime came for her. She was freed from her drab surroundings unto the grandeur of heaven.

• Contemplating our oldest child's departure was distressing until I saw the beginnings of God's perfect will for her future.

Moving Day

The nest on our porch had been the nursery for a finch family. Both parents were clinging to the chain of the porch swing encouraging the fledglings to take their first flight. Mr. and Mrs. Finch persistently chirped, "Come on! You can do it! We'll be right behind you!"

Soon, one of the young birds flew the length of the porch and out into a large tree in our yard, while the parents followed. A brother was left alone in the nest until his turn to fly.

Jessica had looked at many colleges and was narrowing her choices. A mainline liberal arts college had come out on top. I dreaded the thought of her departure.

- *I've made too many mistakes!*
- *Is she ready?*
- *Can she stand as a Christian in this world of sin?*
- *Having done absolutely everything together as a family, how can I bear her absence from our circle?*

Within merely a week, the Lord confirmed that 1) she indeed would be ready enough, 2) He was more than able to finish her, and 3) He could easily lift the burden from me.

We are so like the parent finches. We feed our children's minds, spirits and bodies, giving them a strong foundation for the day when they fly the nest. We encourage them with cheers and support. Because we have gone the extra mile to provide the most important basics, we can rest in the assurance that they will be able to complete whatever flights the Lord has planned for them. We can also trust Him to take us on our own flights above the pain of separation.

Letting Go

Damp mist surrounded our mini-van as we drove east through Iowa on I-80. Carload after carload of students from Abraham Lincoln High, on their way to a tournament recklessly sped around us, and each other. Suddenly a student climbed half way out of a vehicle and sat on the window ledge.

Damp mist formed in my eyes as I glanced at Jessica, resting beside me, and thought of Zephi, fifteen, behind. The contrast between our children and those students on that highway confirmed that God did indeed have a special plan for them. In our bubble of a life, we had failed to notice how God had set our children apart.

> Jessica, 20, graduated from the Bible college the Lord chose for her with a diploma in General Church Leadership.

We had almost missed our meeting with destiny. I had not wanted to make the two-thousand mile trip to visit the Bible college. Then God spoke in His still, small voice (1 Kin. 19:12) and confirmed His plan, letting me know that the trip would enable His perfect will for Jessica and protect her from a life lived outside of that will.

- *I wept quietly behind our drapes when a dear neighbor saw her daughter onto the yellow school bus for the first time.*
- *I peacefully sat on our porch swing and watched our half-grown daughters walk down the street to their first baby-sitting job.*
- *Now I confidently rest in knowing that God has provided this stepping stone into life, a safe place for Jessica to finish growing up.*

We are not perfect parents. We have not had a perfect school—far from it! Yet, by God's mercy and grace, our young adults are not like those teenagers we saw that day on that highway.

✫ **There is a time and season for everything. We must let go and allow the Lord to shepherd our older children, trusting that He will guide them into His perfect plan.**

Does the Mom Make the Child?

Be sober, be vigilant; because your adversary the devil, as a roaring lion, walketh about, seeking whom he may devour. Whom resist stedfast in the faith . . . (1 Pet. 5:8,9).

Andrea Yates thought she was a terrible mother. She didn't want her children to go to hell, so she murdered them. Andrea loved her children. She told authorities that her motive for their murder was to spare them from worse evil. Andrea was victimized by the devil's lies and his tools of mind altering drugs. "The Murderer"—whose quest is to be like the Most High (Is. 14)—placed in Andrea's heart the thought that she was as God; that her children's salvation depended on her alone.

This philosophy—that we make our children—reveals our lack of knowledge of God. (Hos. 4:6) The Lord God Almighty is the only one who knows the end from the beginning. Just because the beginning or the middle looks bad doesn't mean that the life won't end well, that the child won't end up a godly, mature adult. People change. They mature, and there is always the life-changing miracle of Genuine Salvation.

> God is much bigger than any of us can comprehend.

Since we don't see the end from here, we have no right to think that our failings will ruin our children. This is putting much too much importance on self and off of God.

Andrea Yates did not believe God's Salvation was enough. She felt she had to take the punishment for her failings upon herself. This is wrong. Christ is our righteousness. (Gal. 2:16) Our own righteousness is totally worthless. Only when we kneel before our Maker, confessing our inadequacy, will he make us adequate in Him. We really should do this daily. We need to lean more heavily on the everlasting arms in these days, when the devil walketh about so aggressively seeking our children—the ones who have been set apart for Him. ☆ **These particular children are just the ones who will do the most damage to the kingdom of darkness. This is why there has been a hard struggle for some of us.**

Even if all appears well in your childrens' lives, keep vigilant, always pray. I know from experience that years can go by with seemingly no struggles. Then the enemy appears, ready to pull a child over the precipice to hell. The devil is a liar!

We need to learn spiritual warfare—the warfare on our knees for our childrens' souls. We need to be vigilant—knowing the enemy's ways and God's will for protection and deliverance through His Word. We need to discern the works of the enemy before undue damage is done, taking the authority

> Know that your labour is not in vain in the Lord.
>
> *1 Cor. 15:58*

that Jesus gave us, fully empowered by knowledge of the Scriptures and resulting faith. And yes, we need to add our labor in the Lord to our faith and do right. ☆ **Even if it looks hopeless, remember—we walk by faith, not sight. God is always greater, always good and always wants good for His children—our children.**

"Mother"—A Tribute

Muffled sobs startled me. I lifted my head to my mother's tear-stained cheeks. Soon my five-year-old eyes also began to fill with tears as *her* mother's coffin was lowered into place. She hugged me to herself. Little did we know, on the other end of life's long road, our hearts would again be knit in grief.

Throughout the years, Mom's cheery, outgoing personality nurtured and kept our family close. Although she worked and had many friends, neither took priority over her family or her meticulous homemaking. To both family and friends she modeled optimism, charity, tolerance, flexibility and contentedness, accepting whatever came her way. She never complained about her "lot in life" nor was she ever sick. Her faith kept her well.

Springtime in the Rockies

My dad's deep and pleasant voice resounded from his six foot, two inch frame as we drove home from Grandma's in our black Ford. Before the distraction of radio, we made the miles fly by singing together as a family. He sang to five foot, two inch Mom:

When it's springtime in the Rockies,
I'll be coming home to you,
Little Sweetheart of the mountains,
With your bonnie eyes so blue.

Once again, I'll say I love you,
As the birds sing all the day,
Little sweetheart of the mountains,
Of the mountains far away.[2]

and . . .

When your hair has turned to silver,
I will love you as today,
I will always call you sweetheart,
That will always be your name.

Through the garden filled with roses,
Down the sunset aisle we'll stray.
When your hair has turned to silver,
I will love you as today.[3]

Down life's road, I looked at Mom and her hair was silver, and they were still together, although they had more than their share of troubles. Even tremendous difficulties did not hinder Mom's faith in God, others and herself. During stressful times, this amazing woman comforted others and assured them that all would be well. When her second husband died, instead of focusing on her own loss, she immediately and regularly began visiting nursing homes.

Mom lived to give. She loved to give. She wanted to give. It gave her joy to give, but one day, many years after that day at the cemetery, she had nothing to give. They took away her money, her possessions and her rights.

One day, soon after confinement, the nursing home staff let me take her out the door. They had not been informed of the legal restrictions. The courts would not allow her to live with us as we desired, nor allow us to take her out, even for holidays.

Mom said that gray day was beautiful. Oh, that I could have driven to the moon! I was forced by law to take her back to the home they put her in. The normally energetic woman was so heavily drugged she could hardly walk. This woman—who chose young friends and could never relate to "old people"—saw the stooped bodies in wheel chairs, started shaking uncontrollably, dropped her head and cried. My eyes filled with tears as I held her close.

I am tempted to say I will never be half the mother she was to me. When I look at how I measure up, the lack in my own motherhood is overwhelming. My only hope as a mother is the Christ who lives within me, making me the mother He wants me to be by His Word and His Spirit. He is more than enough.

On February 10, 1999, after two and one half years behind locked doors, Mom was presented with sweet freedom and fresh new life. The places she loved on this earth—and longed to see again—pale into dingy monochrome in view of the eternal and exquisitely beautiful springtime that she is experiencing now. No more tears, no more chains—hallelujah! The following ballad describes her faith-filled, optimistic, cheerful and fun-loving personality and is my tribute to her.

Farewell

Farewell!—but whenever you welcome the hour
That awakens the night-song of mirth in your bower,
Then think of the one who once welcomed it too,
And forgot her own griefs to be happy with you.
Griefs may return, not a hope may remain

Of the few that have brightened the pathway of pain;
But we'll never forget the short vision that threw
Its enchantment around us, while lingering with you.

And still on that evening, when pleasure fills up,
To the highest top sparkle each heart and each cup,
Where'er my path lies, be it gloomy or bright,
My soul, happy friends, shall be with you that night;
Shall join in your revels, your sports and your wiles,
And return to me beaming all o'er with your smiles—
Too blest, if it tells me that, 'mid the gay cheer,
Some kind voice had murmured, "I wish she were here!"

Let Fate do her worst; there are relics of joy,
Bright dreams of the past which time can't destroy;
Which come in the night-time of sorrow and care,
And bring back the features that joy used to wear.
Long, long be my heart with such memories filled!
Like the vase, in which roses have once been distilled—
You may break, you may shatter the vase if you will,
But the scent of the roses will hang round it still.[4]

Thomas Moore (1779-1852)

Moore had a genius for friendship. Byron, who described
him as the most pleasing individual he had ever met,
begged for his companionship when in exile. . . . In turn,
Moore reveled in the company of others as much as they in
his, as evident in this touching threnody on the sadness of
separation from those he loves.[5]

Moore, in fact, was very much like Mom.

•◦ List those good things you have learned from your mother. Then follow her example and apply her teaching to your own mothering and homemaking.

The Century's Turning Point

A survey tagged the 1950s as the most favored decade of the 20th century. Standing alone as a time of both normalcy and prosperity, these years draw us rearward. Problems were few and far between, but this very same era initiated a scourge upon society with the introduction and subsequent habitual use of the television. Upon this "box" morality pivoted and the "good life" began to spiral downward.

Before TV? From the mid 1800s to the early 1900s my great-grandparents and my grandparents joined with other musicians and families for old-country dances. "Polish people may not have had a lot of material goods when they arrived in America, but they brought their independent spirit and a love of folk music and dancing."[6]

Our tiny village had its own orchestra and the music of John Philip Sousa reverberated from the park's gazebo bandstand. When the very first train screeched to a halt on June 4, 1886, the whole town greeted it. Some joined the dignitaries on board and rumbled on down the track to the next town.[7]

Work was the lifeblood of that time and brought blessing on succeeding generations. People balanced their daily dose of good hard labor with church, neighbors and occasional social gatherings.

As a child I spent summers on my uncle's farm. During the week, my cousins and I helped wherever needed and worked on projects and presentations for the county fair. On Saturday evenings, we went to town and watched free open-air movies from benches in an empty lot. Back home in the "city" my parents alternated hosting Friday night get-togethers with two uncles and their families. This stopped rather abruptly when we, along with many other Americans, became the proud owners of a new and "wondrous" invention—the television.

No longer was there a need to interact with others. Social structure became age-segregated and shallow—children at school, parents at work. Creativity and literacy were squelched. Television became the center of the family, sometimes taking the place of the father in influence and authority.

Some say TV was good in its early days, with programs such as "Ozzie and Harriet," but the early days also started the long line of comedies that degrade man, who is made in God's image. A local paper called Audrey Meadows of "The Honeymooners," "one of television's strongest, most spirited wives." Ms. Meadows' own life was congruent with television's path downward. She was born in China to missionary parents (and probably raised in schools apart from them as was the practice). She then debuted as a soprano at Carnegie Hall, performed light opera, acted on Broadway and finally became a sketch comedienne on television. Her character on "The Honeymooners" modeled rebellion to American women. This was a seed, among others, that has grown into a noxious weed, choking the joy of femininity—*a meek and quiet spirit, which is in the sight of God of great price* (1 Pet. 3:4).

> I'm not asking you, Ralph, I'm telling you!
>
> *The Honeymooners*

TV portrays and indoctrinates acceptance of behavior and lifestyles that are abominable to God. It is a behavior modification tool, a mind- and spirit-dulling drug. Many Americans admit that morality is on a downward spiral. Moral and ethical problems arise from a departure from "the fear of the Lord." A departure from God has been nurtured by the devilish influences of TV.

Butter and honey shall he eat, that he may know to refuse the evil, and choose the good (Is. 7:15). Our precious children need to be shielded from evil at every age. They need to learn that there is a gulf between the holy and the profane. Keeping TV out of our homes will help teach this, and enable a fuller blessing in every area. In addition, your children will respect you more for making godly choices about TV.

✗ If your husband wants television, do not take a hammer to it! While he is viewing, spend time in quiet devotions with your children. Meanwhile, pray television out of your house, and it will soon be out. Continue to pray to keep it out.

Video and Children

Want to teach your children the ways of the world, the flesh and the devil? Want to make them weak-willed in the face of sin? Want to mold a mindset that cannot discern right from wrong, perhaps one that even thinks wrong is right? Want to create violent kids who are apathetic about violence? Want dull-brained children who have no interest in real learning?

Turn on your TV.

Rent another video.

Buy a new electronic game.

Since the 1960s, children have become more difficult to teach. Classes have had to be "dumbed down" with less homework, less challenging material and lower academic standards. Dr. Jennings Bryant of the University of Alabama says viewing reduces vigilance, which is the ability to remain actively focused on a task. One early study on the effects of TV compared brain waves while reading, to those while watching television. The TV viewing produced alpha waves, indicative of a non-learning brain.

Dr. Jerre Levy, bio-psychologist at the University of Chicago and international authority, feels that older children may be even more affected by the low language content of video. The frontal-lobe development that enables higher-level learning continues throughout childhood and adolescence.

☆ **Some say that with hard work, even very old brains can be changed. This should give us motivation to continue to work with our older children!**

Does your child exhibit any of these characteristics?
- ❏ Difficulty in paying attention
- ❏ Difficulty in expression
- ❏ Struggle with or avoidance of writing assignments
- ❏ Inability to persist in solving problems
- ❏ Inability to read "hard" books
- ❏ Inability to do challenging work

❏ Boredom with "regular" learning
❏ A hypnotic, non-learning state
❏ An under-developed brain
❏ Overstimulation and resulting aggressiveness

Excess video usage robs the child of the brain stimulation and growth that result from reading. Even pictures in books can hinder learning. Arthur Woodward of the University of Rochester claims that visuals drastically weaken text.

While reading, children create mental pictures of the characters—what they look like, what they are feeling, what tone of voice they are speaking in, what the environment looks like and what the environment feels like. In other words, the child's brain works at creativity, giving it the exercise it needs to develop properly. The brain actually branches with these activities, expanding its capacity. The brain needs to:

• Think
• Solve problems
• Listen
• Figure out story lines

Such a brain is able to "talk" to itself, instantly sending messages from one area to another. Efficiency (of the brain) is developed only by active practice in thinking and learning which in turn builds increasingly stronger connections.[8]

✔ Dr. Jane Healy Ph.D., author of *Endangered Minds*, echoes Charlotte Mason in saying that an effective way to probe a reader's understanding is to ask him to tell what happened or to give a summary or paraphrase of his reading.

Subtlety

By Jean Hall

I am not impressed by parents who crack their voices like a whip or roll an evil eye towards an erring child. The best child trainers are those whose children behave in public. Yet, if misbehavior breaks out, their correction is almost imperceptible.

Our children and their friends were galloping pretend horses up and down the sidewalk, shouting and hitting them with pretend sticks and jerking at the reins. Here was a golden opportunity to introduce six-year-old Genevieve to some reality.

I explained that the very best horse trainers handled their horses so well that sometimes you would not even see their signals. I showed her how to hold the reins, how to loosen them and lean forward to signal the horse to go faster, how to pull slightly and sit up straight to tell your horse to slow down, how to barely tighten the reins with a twitch of your wrist to "collect" the horse and prepare it to receive a new command or direction. She was interested to hear that repeated jerking of the reins or pulling at the horse's mouth makes for a hard-mouthed, less responsive animal. She then took off on her stick-horse. It was interesting to watch her practice flexing her wrists slightly, rather than jerking the reins of her trusty steed.

Child training has its similarities. Children grow used to raised voices, nasty faces and jerks on the heart. They will soon not respond to a mild tone or the slightly lifted eyebrow. It takes effort to avoid venting annoyance and to remain calm and cheerful, yet I have seen a difference in our own children's responsiveness by practicing subtlety and consistency.

Abiding in His Grace

By Teresa Jennings Robinson

Come unto me, all ye that labour and are heavy laden, and I will give you rest. Take my yoke upon you, and learn of me; for I am meek and lowly in heart: and ye shall find rest unto your souls. For my yoke is easy, and my burden is light (Matt. 11:28-30).

It was a time in my life when every day was overwhelming at best, crippling at worst. My days often ended with a combination of tears and exhaustion. One morning, I began to weep uncontrollably after reading the words of Jesus in Matthew 11:28-30. It was as though I was reading those gentle words for the very first time. The Presence of the Lord filled the rooms of my heart and home, illuminating the dark despair and wrapping the pain with His grace.

The Lord was beckoning me to rest in Him—to cease striving and allow Him to order my day. He revealed the areas of my life that needed to be transformed and more completely surrendered to Him. I had unknowingly placed more trust in my ability to manage than in God's plan for my life. Somewhere between juggling my responsibilities as bride, mother, home manager, as well as care-giver to ailing family members, I had allowed schedules and expectations to replace the assurance that God's Grace was sufficient—always and no matter what.

It was at that instant I began to see that running as fast as I could each day was not the way to accomplish what the Lord had called me to do. From the moment I awoke each morning until I lay my head down at night, I moved from one activity to another, tending to the seemingly countless responsibilities of my life. Even my quiet time with the Lord had simply become another item on my never-ending "To-Do" list. I had moved from surrendering to controlling—spinning my proverbial wheels as I toiled over every decision.

If His burden is light and His yoke is easy, what was weighing me down? I had taken on the yoke of perfectionism; I was bowing to the expectations of others. I was carrying unnecessary baggage and the burden of being the perfect wife, mother and homemaker in order to live up to some imaginary list of demands—my own list being the most burdensome. I had fallen into the trap of believing that I had to model everyone else's life instead of living the life God had designed for me. It was a turning point for me.

I decided to allow God to order my day, to cease striving in my futile attempt to be perfect. The solution was to abide in His Perfect Grace for my every need and to seek Him first in all things.

✫ I realized scheduling time for God was not the same as abiding in Him. Abiding is not a single act; it is consistently yielding one's heart to hear the voice of God as He provides comfort and direction. It is to relinquish control and trust in Him.

For more on abiding in Christ, see Chapter 9, "Producing Fruit."

One More Exact Translation

While Madison Avenue proliferates Bible versions that have precious people poorly edified and informed, the devil snickers about how his plan is progressing. He is not afraid of some insignificant essay like this, when millions (both Christian and not) are flowing with the current to the culmination of his eternal goal to be like the most High. (Is. 14:14) Pastors replace *King James Version* pew Bibles with the *New International Version*, preach its superiority, read their sermons from books, remove old hymnals and then are subsequently removed themselves—but not until many wounded and dying saints are left by the wayside.

The Fruit

- Christians are not walking in the abundance that Christ came to give His own.
- Christians run not only to physicians, but also to psychologists and psychiatrists. This is a spirit of the times: having utmost faith in the so-called experts—mere men with professional titles.
- Learning and wisdom lessen in children and adults.
- Adults walk less and less in the power of God, even to the point of not being able to stand in faith for their own family's needs. *. . . faith cometh by hearing, and hearing by the word of God* (Rom. 10:17).
- New Age thinking permeates our churches. Apostate Christians grow closer to New Agers in doctrines and beliefs.

Are we wasting the precious few years, hours and minutes that God has given us on this earth seeking scraps of solutions from here and there? Is it any wonder that there is disagreement among the body at all levels, when we do not have one definitive rule book? The deceit of the translations is so subtle it is unnoticed by most Christians but is preparing them and the world for one world religion and government.

When examined under the scrutiny of the Holy Spirit's righteous, unerring eye, all the other contenders vaporize, leaving only one left standing—the unequaled Authorized *King James Version.*

> *Which now with all humility, we present unto Your Majesty. For when Your Highness had once out of deep judgment apprehended how convenient it was, that out of the Original Sacred Tongues together with comparing of the labours, both in our own and other foreign languages, of many men who went before us, there should be* **one more exact translation** *of the holy Scriptures into the exact tongues.*[9]

For many more reasons to use the KJV, see *New Age Bible Versions* by Gail Riplinger. Even the author was astonished to unearth facts about the deception and intentional changes in the versions.

Living in the Last Days

"We are in that sliver between time and eternity, mortality and immortality, the now and forever!" I put the ministry letter down as this ponderous thought rolled across my mind. Later we listened in rapt attention to a tape. The man said that the temple mount was actually north of the Dome of the Rock. The temple could be rebuilt as a tent at any time and the sacrifices could begin within a few days. The longtime pastor and student of prophecy—although calling his teaching theory—used the Bible to describe the antichrist. He made time predictions based on historical dates and feasts. Other authors and teachers say that the antichrist is alive on this earth right now!

These teachings set our hearts to wondering and searching the Scriptures. The signs are all around us. His return is more real to me, because I lived some fulfilled prophecy within the confines of my own family (Matt. 10:21; 2 Tim. 3:1-3). The Bible says that although the day will come as a thief in the night, it also says: *But ye, brethren, are not in darkness, that that day should overtake you as a thief* (1 Thess. 5:4).

If Jesus is really coming soon, the focus of our life, our days and our homeschools seems obvious. We need to be tightening up our curriculum to envelop our days in eternally important pursuits.

Who then is a faithful and wise servant, whom his lord hath made ruler over his household, to give them meat in due season? Blessed is that servant, whom his lord when he cometh shall find so doing (Matt. 24:45,46).

Teaching for the Last Days

1) *Teach the pure and powerful Word of God.* (Heb. 4:12; Ps. 29:4) The Word will bring faith to overcome situations that are really impossible to overcome otherwise. We must be memorizing the Word with our children. The *King James Version* makes this much easier because of its lovely and expressive English. Teach your children to love the Law by setting aside a quiet time for each to read, study and take notes on what the Lord is teaching them personally. Monitor this discipline at first and occasionally thereafter.

2) *Learn from respected teachers and preachers,* in person, and through their tapes, videos, books and manuals. Make sure your teacher is preaching the pure Word, and preaching much of it. You do not need man's words at a time like this. Be especially wary of those who spend a great deal of time in criticism— definitely unscriptural and of the flesh. *By this shall all men know that ye are my disciples, if ye have love one to another* (John 13:35).

3) *Teach how to praise.* God inhabits His praises, and brings victory in impossible situations through praise. Learn hymns and songs, urging your children to keep their hearts and minds focused on the Lord.

4) *Study historical Christians* who were mighty in faith. If they could do feats of faith, so can we!

5) *Learn and teach old-fashioned skills* such as gardening, seed saving, cooking, food preservation and construction.

I asked my husband if we will need earthly skills and knowledge to judge the world and angels (1 Cor. 6:2, 3) and he said, "Ask the Lord." So right then and there I prayed aloud about it and a few days later God answered with one of my favorite scriptures in His still small voice: *The wisdom of this world is foolishness with God* (1 Cor. 3:19).

How absurd to think the limited knowledge we gain here will be necessary when we have the eternal wisdom of God. The knowledge that is so important to the world for the 21st Century is least important for us.

However, since we don't know exactly when our Lord will return, we should continue with the basics, including computer and typing, but never forgetting that spiritual preparation is much more important than any other subject. Faith will get us through when nothing else can. *For whatsoever is born of God overcometh the world: and this is the victory that overcometh the world, even our faith* (John 5:4).

Reaching Back for the Best

To meet or beat public-school standards, all we have to do is teach our kids to read and write with passable accuracy by the time they are eighteen. . . . We need to start raising our standards. . . . a more challenging and worthwhile standard would be "as good as the schools in the rest of the

world," or "as good as the best kids in our own schools
several decades ago."[10]

I was one of those good students several decades ago, but I would
never consider myself well-educated. Why not reach back a bit
farther to the time when all students were good students? The
decades around the turn of the century produced the most univer-
sally well-educated people. They spent few years in school, but
exited with more knowledge than today's older graduate. Bolstered
by godly values, excellence was expected. Time was not wasted.
Subjects were learned well the first time. High quality books were
the tools of that golden age.

Consider the 1899 edition of *Hoenshel's Advanced Grammar.*
It was written for sixth, seventh and eighth grades and includes
modes, cardinals, ordinals and diagraming. Today, the student who
uses this book may know more than college students—possibly even
more than college professors.

"This book opened many doors for me."[11] The elderly lady spoke
of reading *A Child's History of England* by Dickens, when eight
years old. We also used this book, but it was soon obvious that our
ten- and twelve-year old boys were having difficulty with it so I
assigned it to our thirteen- and fifteen-year-old beginning high
schoolers.

If children have feasted on classic literature from an early age,
they will have no problem with deeper books. In some cases a fast
from chaff may be necessary, to create an appetite for the mentally
nutritious literary germ. From experience (both ways), we know the
following to be true.

Light, frivolous reading brings the brain into a condition
where it is almost impossible for it to grasp and hold
serious matter. When the girl who only reads serial novels
undertakes to read anything that requires thought, she will
at first not comprehend a thing. She will complain that the
book is not interesting, and see nothing in it. But let her
keep at the more serious reading, going over it till she does

*understand it. She will in time become able to grasp most
of the thoughts as she reads. And if she keeps on at the
deeper reading, she will lose her appetite for the light stuff;
it will seem chaffy and foolish to her.*[12]

✔ So how can we, who ran with the likes of Dick and Jane, impart
excellence to our children? Some lofty companions with impeccable
English can compensate for our lack of expertise. The authors and
characters of our greatest books will aid us in our quest for quality in
our educating. Think real classics and forget quasi-classics, the
dumbed-down newer books from the 1950s to 1970s. Do not be
concerned if the only copies that you can find are falling apart.
Instead, thank the Lord that you have those, and use them.

See more about returning to the excellence of the past in Chapter 6, "Raising the
Standard."

Psychiatry in Education[13]

In the late 1800s, Wilhelm Wundt founded experimental psychology
on the premise that—because it could not be measured—the soul or
psyche did not exist. Later, Sigmund Freud expanded this thesis,
which resulted in the demise of religion, and in the growth of
promiscuity. Meanwhile, certain Wundtian disciples were making a
more direct assault on education.

James Earl Russell, Dean and Head of the Department of
Psychology at Columbia University Teachers' College, recruited
Edward Lee Thorndike and John Dewey to join him and by 1899 the
college promoted psychological courses for all teachers. In 1925
more than a thousand schools began curriculum revision based on
their new philosophy. Just as the corruption of the Bible was intentional,[14] the dumbing down of education was also planned. John
Dewey claimed that teaching children to read was a "great perver-
sion" and that a high literacy rate bred "destructive" individualism.

Thorndike wrote in 1929 that " . . . the program of the average
elementary school is too narrow and academic in character. . . .

Subjects such as arithmetic, language, and history include content that is intrinsically of little value. . . . " He later revealed his goal of controlling human nature. At this time, government and the mental health industry—through conferences and reports—began promoting psychiatry's goals. In 1948, the co-founder of the World Federation for Mental Health said:

> The only lowest common denominator of all civilizations and the only psychological force capable of producing these perversions (such as guilt) is morality, the concept of right and wrong. . . . We have swallowed all manner of poisonous certainties fed us by our parents . . . and others. . . . The results . . . are frustration, inferiority, neurosis and inability to enjoy living, to reason clearly or to make a world fit to live in.

In 1950, a White House Conference on Education promoted counseling services for all students. In 1961, the report, "Action for Mental Health," proposed that school curriculum be designed "to bend the student to promote mental health . . . as a means of altering culture." The National Institute of Mental Health reinforced this view and redefined education as "teaching people to behave as they do not behave, rather than teaching them to know what they do not know."

The "Experts"

Just who are these "experts" who mold children's souls? Psychiatrists have a suicide rate three times higher than the general population. Ten percent admit to having committed sexual offenses with patients. One study reports that two-thirds of them are seriously mentally ill themselves.

What is the result of their meddling with minds? A populace that once cut its teeth on the works of Lincoln, Jefferson, Cicero and Aristotle is now in front of the TV, totally ignorant of its own culture, heritage and human potential. Education now consists of values clarification, sensitivity training, encounter groups, self-esteem training and mastery learning. These OBE (outcome-based education) tools are changing "the thoughts, feelings and actions of children."[15]

With no standards, is it any wonder we see violence among students? Arkansas was one of the first states to introduce OBE. One school there presented films showing an ax-wielding young man, a man drowning with his feet in a cement block and rows of dead bodies. A result of messing with minds in that state? Murder and mayhem at Western Middle School.

Witchcraft is an expression of man's rebellion against God. . . . Its driving force is to control people and circumstances. To gain this end it may use either psychological pressures or psychic techniques or a combination of both.[16]

2

Pursuing Better Parenting

The feelings are to be disciplined; the passions are to be restrained; true and worthy motives are to be inspired; profound religious feeling is to be instilled; and pure morality inculcated under all circumstances. All this is comprised in education.

Daniel Webster

*T*here comes a day when every Christian parent realizes ☆ **the most important aim in parenting is not an educated child, but a godly child.** That day is a sad one if the parents have failed to live the example their child needs, or if they have led the child in the pursuit of knowledge while neglecting spiritual training or even if they have failed to train proper habits, which reflect a life ordered by God.

Children learn more from family relationships, attitudes, structure and systems than from any teaching. Knowing this, the priority is to build godly systems into our homes, and high character into our own lives. In this chapter we will look at systems and structure. In Chapter 9, we will learn to produce spiritual fruit in order to be the example our children need. Because we pursue better parenting now, our children will mature into adults who bring glory to Him and joy to us. He will then say, *Well done, thou good and faithful servant* (Matt. 25:21).

I made many mistakes in parenting. Although I cannot return to the days when my children were most responsive and teachable, *you* can learn from my experiences. You do not have to make my mistakes. I have walked through these challenges so I can "preach" more forcefully what I share in this chapter. My failures can be your successes, if you listen and do what God tells you to do. Although I must now lean on His grace for my young adults, you can do as He directs with your younger children.

Jonathan Edwards wrote, "Family education and order are some of the chief means of grace; if these are duly maintained, all the means of grace are likely to prosper and become effectual." Your efforts will bring forth a sure reward.

Christianity vs. Humanism

There is far too much humanism in today's parenting and it is not working. This humanism lifts the child up as his own authority. Humanism says:

- *Don't you dare cross the child's will.* The truth is that will-training brings the child into dominion over himself as he bows to the dominion of God. This very training produces peace, order and productivity.

- *They are children only once; don't make them work so hard.* Actually, hard work is crucial in building a responsible adult. We are to train our children to work, not as a taskmaster over slaves, but—ideally—as partners in labor.

- *Who are you, Parent, thinking you can control another human being?* We must take authority over our children as God's representatives on earth. He wills it. The result of proper child training is a blessed life and a glorious eternity for both child and parent.

• *Chastising a child is cruel.* The truth is that godly chastisement will keep the child from the cruelty of hell and from a hellish life on earth.

Separation vs. Socialization

The fact that humanism is ingrained in our culture, requires separation. Just as the early Christians separated themselves from the esteemed philosophies of the Greeks and Romans, we must also separate ourselves. (2 Cor. 6) It is especially imperative that our children be kept from the influential ideas of this age. Is this not why we have chosen homeschooling?

If your child spends much time with a friend who is educated in public schools, what philosophy will he be assimilating? This relationship may result in an upheaval of the Christian family and a warring within the child. The child, especially when older, may even begin to unknowingly side with humanism, saying things like, "I can do what I want," or "You can't tell me what to do."

Do not let your children go anywhere, at any age, without God's sure guidance. Do not let them go anywhere, at any age, without your own close guidance; or without transferring that authority to another trusted individual, such as a godly spouse when they marry. This is the ideal—however, God is big enough to take good care of our children even if they leave home outside of these guidelines. He is also able to return them to His perfect plan for their lives, should they go their own way.

An exception is marriage out of God's will. Your child must avoid this life sentence which would affect even your grandchildren. Pray earnestly and regularly from an early age that God will send His choice to your child. If it is already too late, if your child has married wrongly, God can still change the relationship by changing the individuals. It will take a miracle, but with God all things are possible. (Matt. 19:26; Mark 9:23, 10:27, 14:36)

Separation from the world (2 Cor. 6:17) should be separation unto the family, and unto the family of God. Do not allow separation

> **Limit the time your child spends alone.**

unto self. This displays itself in much time alone in rooms or elsewhere and breeds an independent, self-willed child. An hour or two alone each day should be sufficient. Keep family time fun. Fill your days with family activities such as interactive devotions, work projects, study, reading aloud, games, visits, hobbies and cooking so that the children want to be with the family. Even if the child does not wish it, it should be required. Even if you do not wish it, you will be thankful that you established routines that draw your family together. When unseen hands begin to pull your older children away, family ambience will keep them connected.

Perfecting Ourselves

Henry Ward Beecher said "Men cannot be developed perfectly who have not been compelled to bring children up to manhood."[1]

Parenting is a formidable challenge, true, but where else would there be so many opportunities to come "unto a perfect man"? (Eph. 4:13) Before we can be effective parents, we must perfect ourselves. I have found this a most difficult task, but we "can do all things" through Christ. We can conquer our wills. We must conquer our wills, if we want success in our child training and educating. "Undisciplined schools and teachers cannot be productive of disciplined students."[2] Our children become what we are. We are their examples (1 Pet. 5:2-4) and yet, the child is also responsible:

> *Your son or daughter responds according to the Godward focus of his or her life. If your child knows and loves God, if your child has embraced the fact that knowing God can enable him to know peace in any circumstance, then he will respond constructively to your shaping efforts. If your child does not know and love God, but tries to satisfy his soul's thirst by drinking from a cistern that cannot hold water (Jer. 2:13), your child may rebel against your best*

*efforts. You must do all that God has called you to do but
the outcome is more complex than whether you have done
the right things in the right way. Your children are responsible for the way they respond to your parenting.*[3]

Systems

The word *system* is defined as *a way of doing things; an orderly
mode of operation governed by general laws or rules.*[4] It is more
abstract than structure (explained later), yet extremely important.

The systems of a house would include heating and cooling,
electricity, sanitation and even family
chores—all those things that create order and
comfort in that dwelling.

I had to have a system while writing
this chapter. Each section had to flow
smoothly to the next, and it didn't come
automatically—I struggled and neglected

> We need
> systems to
> parent
> successfully.

writing for a time because the chapter seemed chaotic. After reread-
ing the introduction several times, I finally discerned that the
chapter was to be divided into the two main topics of systems and
structure. The outline concept and other writing principles were my
rules, according to the definition for the word *systems.*

Without systems we will not see results in the future, nor peace
in the present. Thankfully, we don't need to invent any principles
upon which to base our systems. They are found in the ancient, sure
and enduring Word of God.

The Kingship of God

For the Christian, God is King. The fundamental premise of a godly
family system is that God reigns over the family. The parents are
under God's authority and are His servants. They do all that they do
unto Him and according to His standards (systems). The parents are
to have complete loving command over the children. This authority

does not end when the children turn thirteen, or even eighteen. If there has been consistency (a structural element, more below), the child will recognize that there will always be an authority in their lives and that the parents are that authority, after God, and before marriage. Even after marriage, the child should recognize the parents' greater wisdom and experience, seriously considering their guidance.

Parent, you rule not for your own convenience—although that is a fruit of proper ruling. You need to communicate this to your children. Tell them that their training is not necessarily because you wish it, but because God wills it. Parenting is a holy charge from God that you must accept and fulfill. He has commanded, so you have no choice in the matter. Nor do you need the child's approval or agreement. The children, with repeated exposure to God's word by reading, teaching, preaching, meditation and memorization, watered by the parents' believing prayers and consistency in training, are moved toward perfect submission.

> Your motive should be to please God.

✗ Pray often (at least daily) for your children, but especially for their parents. Because your children become who you are, ☆ **prayer for yourself and for your husband is imperative.** It is even more important if you do not have godly parents, in-laws or others to "stand in the gap." (Ezek. 22:30)

Parenting by the Book

And the LORD, he it is that doth go before thee; he will be with thee, he will not fail thee, neither forsake thee: fear not, neither be dismayed (Deut. 31:8).

"Biblical goals require a biblical approach. . . . "[5] We must guard against molding our training to our own whims, but must allow God's standards to guide us. Each Scripture in the Bible—when followed—enables the Christian family to thrive. Do not revert to "what your parents did" or to what Dr. Laura says. Did you catch the word *revert?* Anything less than God's handbook is less than what you need for this challenging task.

•◆ Search the Scriptures and keep a notebook of what God tells you about parenting. Write special verses, notes, prayers and directions from God. *What thing soever I command you, observe to do it: thou shalt not add thereto, nor diminish from it* (Deut. 12:32). Here are some to start with:

O that there were such an heart in them, that they would fear me, and keep all my commandments always, that it might be well with them, and with their children for ever (Deut. 5:29).

Fearing the Lord—respecting Him as Mighty Creator, Ruler of All, and Judge—results in godly living. When we fear the Lord, we keep His commandments—all of the Word—and are the example we need to be. Don't neglect the early formative years for training in godliness by your example. As your children get older the training will be more difficult. The clay will begin to set. If we don't train our children in the way they should go (Prov. 22:6), they will be set in the way we don't want them to go, and will "not depart from it," without divine intervention.

Come, ye children, hearken unto me: I will teach you the fear of the LORD (Ps. 34:11).

The fear of the Lord is taught by much Word. Spend time in it with your children. Have a Word Routine—daily, nightly, on the Lord's day and so on. Keep it up. Be diligent and consistent to reap a good harvest. *Gather the people together . . . that they may hear, and that they may learn, and fear the LORD your God, and observe to do all the words of this law: And that their children, which have not known any thing, may hear, and learn to fear the LORD your God, as long as ye live . . .* (Deut. 31:12-13).

*W*ives, submit yourselves unto your own husbands, as unto the Lord *(Eph. 5:22).*

As the wife submits humbly to her authorities (God and husband), her children will learn that they must submit to their authorities (God and parents). Our submission will teach our sons as well as our daughters. When they see us respecting their father, whom they love dearly, they will in turn respect us. Both parents should be dedicated to pleasing God first—the husband is not to be the wife's god. All we do for each other should be done as unto the Lord.

*T*rain up a child in the way he should go: and when he is old, he will not depart from it *(Prov. 22:6).*

This doesn't say our children will depart from God's ways for a season and then come back. No "ifs," "ands" or "buts" about it—our children *will not* depart from God's ways. We can and must stand on this anchor Scripture. We must believe it with all our hearts because there may be times when what we see can make us doubt it.

*W*hatsoever a man soweth, that shall he also reap *(Gal. 6:7).*

To get respect from your children, sow respect by showing respect. Show respect to your children by listening to them and treating them with as much kindness as you would show an adult friend or neighbor.

*H*e that ruleth . . . with diligence . . . not slothful in business; fervent in spirit; serving the Lord . . . *(Rom. 12:8, 11).*

Raising children is no game, but the most important thing you will do with your life. This is exactly why—without constant empowerment by the Holy Spirit—it is so difficult. Training and teaching your children is your calling, your charge—and for most mothers—your only ministry, along with the ministry to your husband.

May I speak to fathers also? This refers to you as well. If you do not accept this charge given primarily to fathers, you will regret it deeply someday. Forgive me for being bold and intrusive, but this is crucial and urgent—you have so few years before your children leave to live their own lives.

*A*nd all thy children shall be taught of the LORD . . . (Is. 54:13).

If we fully realize that the Lord is the teacher, we can relax. Sure, we are not qualified, but He is! Sometimes we just don't know what to do. He does! He will empower us to fulfill the role He's given us. To be taught of the Lord also means to be taught what He deems important. For instance, we must cultivate benevolence for humanity and love for family, neighbors and friends.

*F*athers [and mothers], *provoke not your children to anger, lest they be discouraged . . .* (Col. 3:21).

How would one provoke their children? Here are a few ways:
- Demand obedience.
- Address your children with anger.
- Be unreasonable.
- Let them know you are the authority (pride).
- Criticize them.
- Yell at them.
- Throw things at them.
- Threaten them.
- Hit or slap them.

. . . but bring them up in the nurture and admonition of the Lord (Eph. 6:4).

To nurture means to bring up your children with tender care. Nurture with:

- Love
- Gentleness
- Kindness
- Compassion
- Time and attention
- Loving deeds such as caring for them (cooking, etc.)

Admonish means to warn, notify of a fault, reprove gently and kindly, but seriously. We admonish by correcting with the Word, speaking it all the time, according to Deut. 6:7: *And thou shalt teach them diligently unto thy children, and shalt talk of them when thou sittest in thine house, and when thou walkest by the way, and when thou liest down, and when thou risest up.*

*I*t is good for a man that he bear the yoke in his youth (Lam. 3:27).

Work is good. The result of requiring regular work from a child is peace and maturity as Lamentations continues in verse 28: *He sitteth alone and keepeth silence, because he hath borne it upon him.* Those of my children who were required to work hard from a very young age are extremely responsible adults. The more work (responsibility) they had when young, the more responsible they are as adults. Temper the requirement for work with your example of cheerful and arduous labor. The child should have daily chores from an early age and they should increase in number and complexity as the child matures.

✗ Both mother and child should do the hardest, or least desired, tasks first. With these out of the way, there will be a satisfying sense of accomplishment and a blessing on the rest of the day.

*L*et all bitterness, and wrath, and anger, and clamour, and evil speaking, be put away from you . . . (Eph. 4:31).

"Appeal to the brutal . . . and you develop it; appeal to the noble and you develop that."[6] Nothing can hinder or increase a child's progress more than the prophecies the parents speak over that child. We have all heard the stories of the parent who says to their child, "You are no good and will never amount to anything!" Just as the Lord God created the world by speaking, He will create good in our children by our positive, encouraging, faith-filled words.

✗ Decide that you are going to turn your ranting and complaining and negative talk around. Overcome evil with good and watch the Lord create a new atmosphere in your home. Students want to be efficient and do their best. Positive words stoke these fires. I am reminded of Carol's "Well done," in Karen Andreola's *Pocketful of Pinecones.* Tell your children, "I'm so glad I have such good students!" Instead of berating their messy papers say, "You are doing better every day. I know you will do even better tomorrow."

•• Study the following passages about the creative power of words: Rom. 4:17, 18: 20-21; 2 Cor. 4:13.

A *child left to himself bringeth his mother to shame* (Prov. 29:15).

❏ Do you say, "Just a minute," to a child wanting your attention?
❏ Do the minutes run into many more than just one?
❏ Do you have a passion for something besides your children? In other words, is there a hobby, work or other interest that holds you more than your children do?
❏ Do you have a quiet child, perhaps one that everyone else speaks for, that you haven't bothered to take aside and get to know? This child is being left to himself.
❏ Do your children spend many hours in their rooms, alone, without interaction from you or their father?
❏ Is your child is being "left to himself" as he spends hours in school or preschool?

✗ Be the mother your children need. You do not have to "do it all." Neither a spotless home nor a perfect school is required. Focus on the priorities: God first, family next, personal interests last. Put time with God first in your day, then breakfast, then school or child time. After your duties, personal activities come next, or—on some days— not at all. However, a mom who puts "first things first" will usually have extra time for self and interests. *Whatsoever a man soweth, that shall he also reap* (Gal. 6:7).

*H*is sons made themselves vile, and he restrained them not (1 Sam. 3:13).

We must restrain our children—teaching and training them to live righteously until they leave our sphere of influence and authority. Restraining stipulates that we are to keep them from doing wrong— whatever it takes. Remember we do not have to please the child—we have to please God.

*B*ut if ye be without chastisement, whereof all are partakers, then are ye bastards, and not sons (Heb. 12:8).

"Correction must focus on the fact that God is offended, not the parent—it moves the child back in line with God's will. It is an expression of love. We love them too much to allow them to go or stay out of God's will."[7] Discipline is positive. It creates an inner and permanent control center in the child, setting up guidelines, stan- dards, requirements, tests and measures. Do not be double-minded, being too lenient one day and overbearing the next. Remain consis- tently temperate.

Chastisement is negative but necessary. If you seem to chastise only in anger, bitterness or any other ungodly attitudes, don't do it. This chastisement will do more harm than good. Godly chastisement realizes that the child is not the problem—*we wrestle not against flesh and blood* (Eph. 6:12). Godly chastisement is motivated by obedience to God and care for the child—for their present and future good. Godly chastisement will drive out foolishness, keep the child out of hell and give wisdom. (Prov. 22:15, 23:13, 24, 29:15) Godly chastisement is done in peace, and should include reproof from God's Word.

If you want consistently obedient children, you must expect obedience on the first normally spoken command, every time. This means work on the parent's part, but this job pays well. Soon your children will obey your soft word and family life will be filled with peace, order and ease.

Warning: While chastising is normal and expected, chastising older children can make them more rebellious, especially if they have not had early, proper chastisement. *To every thing there is a season, and a time to every purpose under the heaven . . .* (Eccl. 3:1). Pray much about what you are to do with your children. Listen to God's direction and do what He says. (See "A Difficult Child," below.)

> Godly chastisement is pure training and must be consistent.

If the parents do not correct in obedience to God, they will not see the full measure of God's blessing. *But that ye must turn away this day from following the LORD? and it will be, seeing ye rebel today against the LORD, that tomorrow he will be wroth with the whole congregation of Israel* (Josh. 22:18).

For thy Maker is thine husband; the LORD of hosts is his name; and thy Redeemer the Holy One of Israel . . . (Is. 54:5).

If you have an ungodly husband, be sure to be the example that your children need regarding your relationship with him. As much as possible, serve him, respect him, love him. Your children will respect you more and learn from you as you model these things.

Single mother, you will have to institute structure and spiritual training. You are the head of the family but in a softer, more feminine way. You actually have some advantages. Although you are totally responsible for the training of your children, they are spared the possible negative influence of a sinful husband. The Lord is your provider and always present to guide and protect your family.

Structure

The best school of discipline is home. Family life is God's own method of training the young; and homes are very much what women make them.

S. Smiles

Structure means "an arrangement of parts." It is more concrete than systems, even being defined as "a building." A structure confines and protects.

Lack of structure is usually caused by the inadequate self-discipline of the parent. If you are not watchful, your children may control your family with their words and actions, and yet will come to hate it. They need strong guidelines for self-respect and proper lifelong habits.

Schedule

To build a structure you need a framework. Daily and weekly family schedule is this framework for your structure. Within the framework, you will find specific areas for breakfast, grooming, church, devotions, bedtime, school subjects and any number of other activities. These activities—each in their own "rooms," make up your schedule.

> *In every walk of life, each day and each hour a million invisible hands stretch out to grasp our attention, our time and our thoughts. If we are not protected by a plan, our hours and days are torn to shreds and scattered like withered leaves in our track.*[8]

Scheduling enables the Christian homeschool to run smoothly, and can raise educational standards. A schedule prevents dawdling, creates order and trains the child to be responsible. The child knows that his schedule must be completed before he is free for the day. He must complete the required number of hours and the required amount of work. Scheduling produces more guilt-free time for individual pursuits and is a paramount tool for lifelong achievement.

❀ See instructions for creating a schedule in *Easy Homeschooling Techniques.*

Consistency

Complete your structure with consistency in well-directed effort. Nothing in parenting or schooling will really work, unless there is consistency. Establish basic rules and routines and then be diligent to keep them each day—as if your life depended on it. Your success does.

You cannot really have structure if you do not have consistency. They go hand in hand. There is a big payoff for those who train themselves to be consistent. You will not only have children with good habits and high character, you will find that you have more time each day for rest, relaxation and personal interests. You will also have the peace that comes from knowing you did "first things first."

The parent must hold the child accountable each day, because—if left to itself—the flesh chooses the easy way. When beginning ❀ **habit training**, no matter what age, do not overwhelm. Concentrate on one habit at a time. Once the habits have been set, the nature chooses what it has been trained to do. Thus we see the diligent older child studying on his own, without any intervention from the teacher. Habits to form can be daily straightening of rooms, grooming, completing the day's school work without fail and so on. It is so easy to put off until tomorrow what really needs to be done today. Sooner than you can imagine, there will be no more days left to teach and

> Consistency in scheduling is the one thing I would adhere to most diligently if I had this to do over.

train. The days of influence pass so quickly. You must do right today, so that when you are released from the demands of intensive parenting, you will exit with the assurance that you did your job well.

Parenting Keys

1) Consistent Schedule
2) Unfailing Faith
3) Positive Words
4) Diligent Optimism
5) Bold Determination

Faith is such a big part of success. Translate that faith into uplifting and positive words. Optimism results from living each day in faith—in the assurance that all will turn out well, that each child will fulfill his potential. Determination is never allowing for failure. It ties all the other keys together. It is the character quality that says, "I will never give up."

Especially for Young Men

Our daughters and our sons need high standards. If the parents have low expectations, the children will not reach their full God-ordained potential. This section addresses standards for young men in particular.

✔ Study the chapters in the Bible about men of God such as Moses, Joshua, Joseph and Daniel. Memorize key scriptures or passages. Young men need to spend time alone with the Lord to learn to walk in His Spirit, so require additional private meditation and study, with exercises such as writing and copy work.

Standards from Daniel

After Daniel took a stand of faith, God gave him an unusual aptitude for learning, along with ability to interpret dreams and visions. His life resulted in honor and promotion. Which character traits from the book of Daniel do you need to focus on with your sons?

❑ *Skill.* Bright and cunning in knowledge.

❑ *Humility.* Giving glory to God.

❑ *Favor.* Favored by God and man.

❑ *Maturity.* Was favored because of maturity.

❑ *Literacy.* Able to use God's Word in a skillful manner.

❑ *Purity.* No blemish, no faults, no sin.

❑ *Strength.* Mental and emotional.

❑ *Health.* Active, mental health, full of faith.

❑ *Youth.* Eager, talking future not past.

❑ *Appearance.* Neat, clean, well-dressed.

❑ *Education.* Well-versed in every branch of learning.

❑ *Manners.* Respectful of authority, not taking offense.

❑ *Self-Government.* The Word inside controlling the flesh.

Standards from Joseph

The following attributes result from walking with God and are taken from Genesis 39 onward.

- *Prosperity in all things.* Prosperity flowed to those around Joseph downward and upward. He blessed others and they blessed him.

- *Authority.* He was given authority because God was with him and because he submitted to authority. The blessing of Joseph came on all that Potiphar had. Our sons will influence and be a blessing to others.

- *Trustworthiness.* Much will be given to a responsible man. Potiphar gave Joseph complete authority over everything he had, showing complete trust.

- *Respect and desire.* Potiphar's wife desired Joseph. Women desire and respect strong men—men with dreams, visions,

power, faith, gentleness, self-control and authority. Your young
man needs a wife who desires and respects him.

- *Freedom.* Even in jail, the Lord was with Joseph and showed
  him mercy. God had a plan for his freedom.
- *Promotion.* The Lord extended Joseph's authority to those in the
  prison.
- *Faith.* In Genesis 40, verse 8, Joseph believed God for the
  interpretation of dreams.
- *Fearless truthfulness.* Joseph was not afraid to tell the chief
  baker his destiny. (40:19)
- *Humility.* Joseph told Pharaoh that the interpretation is not of
  him, but of God. (41:16)
- *Wisdom and discretion.* When famine was imminent, Joseph
  gave wise counsel to Pharaoh. (41:33)
- *The fear of the Lord.* Joseph did not want to kill or take revenge
  on his brothers because he feared God. (42:18)

✔ Do similar studies with your daughters on the women of the Bible,
such as Esther.

A Difficult Child

*Even the captives of the mighty shall be taken away, and the prey
of the terrible shall be delivered: for I will contend with him that
contendeth with thee, and I will save thy children* (Is. 49:25).

Dealing with difficult situations may not be pleasant, but *not*
dealing with them will cause much greater pain to both child and
parent. Have you failed to train your child to have dominion over
himself under God? Older children sometimes display more independent traits than are acceptable. Is your child waiting for the day
when he will leave so that he can "do what he wants"? Is your heart
breaking because your child wants to be free from you? Perhaps
humanistic education or influence has left your dear son or daughter
progressively negative toward all authority. He or she might be
believing the devil's lies that independence equals freedom.

If we have been personifying the schoolmaster with the hickory stick, perhaps it is now time to follow the ideas of Charlotte Mason more closely. She believed that the teacher-parent was to not be the center of the school. Children generally want to do right, and must stand or fall by their own efforts. Do not prod them. Established schedule helps here. It is better that they suffer the consequences of not doing their work, than that they be forced to do it. What good can come from an exasperated mother, urging and prodding, threatening and berating? There needs to be definite, but kind firmness. Our children must learn to choose right, not be forced to do right. This is the end of education. *Now the end of the commandment is charity out of a pure heart, and of a good conscience, and of faith unfeigned . . .* (1 Tim. 1:5).

> **Do not allow the child to form the habit of needing prodding.**

Keep the faith for your young people. God's plan is still in place. His mercy hovers over them. Keep believing and speaking good over them. God can certainly turn a seemingly bad situation to good, and He will, according to your faith and your willingness to turn certain things around in your own life and in your child training. The most important catalyst for change is believing prayer. We have seen many of the following ideas work with our own children.

1) Love, love, love. (Overcome evil with good.)

2) Do not judge.

3) Believe and speak only good about that child.

4) Never use the "R" words (rebel, rebellion, rebellious) referring to that child, especially in his hearing.

5) Praise much.

6) Teach the Bible. Require a number of verses from Proverbs to be read each day. It is a good idea to have your child copy what they read into a notebook, until a sure habit is formed. Make sure they date each day's entry. Check daily at first and then weekly.

7) Cut off or limit contact with certain friends, situations and locations. These will be easy to recognize, as your child's behavior will be different after these encounters. The child is always

being taught, either good or bad. It is always easier to lose than gain ground.

8) Increase time with parents and other godly adults. Young men should spend much time with their fathers.

9) Believe God. Speak the Word in prayer out loud. Speak God's wonderful promises such as Ps. 138:8, 55:22; Eph. 6:12-13; Matt. 16:19; Luke 10:19 and 2 Cor. 10:4.

•• Compile a written list of actions and consequences. Below is an example. Your list can be more appropriate for your child. Even if you have failed to be consistent in the past, be consistent now. Unless you know you will be consistent, do not show this list to your child.

Action → Consequence or Reward

Finishes school on time.   → Afternoon free for projects.
School not finished.   → Dishes, plus school completion.
Keeps room clean.   → New item or decor for room.
Is disrespectful.   → Extra chore or restriction.
Mows lawn.   → Payment or privilege.

Two Moms Suggest
Solutions with Older Children

With my twelve- and thirteen-year-old boys, my decision has been to step back and drastically limit my influence. I have found that we now are applying what we have been learning about for years—not only the 3Rs but the moral, ethical and historical aspects of what we have learned. The amazing transformation of watching them grow into adults has led me to believe it is time for me, as an authority figure, to step back. The boys are at such a time in their life where outside influences will be observed and weighed more heavily and their ultimate decisions I can only hope will be made with some consideration of the knowledge we have imparted over the last years. There will be mistakes and they must learn from these with real world consequences, not just punishment meted out by Mom or Dad. Our ultimate hope is that they will return to us for guidance and advice and be discerning in their judgment.

Janet Barber

If he wants to run his own life, he should be able to pay for it too. That means a job. If he has an idea of a future career, perhaps an apprenticeship is appropriate. School needs to be considered as well and that will mean a list of weekly tasks. He is allowed to set his time-table on those but they must be finished by Friday afternoon at 5:00. I would require a bedtime and if a curfew gets forgotten, the bedtime will come all the earlier the next night. Hopefully his father is involved in these decisions as well and plans for weekend bonding with his son(s).

Priscilla Blanchard

For more parenting help see ☞ **No Greater Joy Ministries.**

Manly Independent Boys

That which makes noble, independent men is of the same stuff that makes manly independent boys: To work and struggle through hardships and privations, knowing in one's secret heart that these are angels in disguise; to bravely, nobly, joyfully fight life's battles as they come; to inhale , like bracing air, the inspiration of a purpose enthroned in the soul; and finally, in the fullness of manhood, to gradually emerge from creek and shoal, free and independent, out upon the high seas of life, with your craft, small but seaworthy, your iron will for a rudder to which it readily responds; your mature judgment for a compass; your horizon of possibility broad as the curves of the earth;

*your freedom only limited by the shores of the ocean; what
inspiration in the thought! what effort it is not worth!
Truly, it is a great thing to be a man!*[9]

Finally

*Although my house be not so with God; yet he hath made with me
an everlasting covenant, ordered in all things, and sure . . .* (2 Sam.
23:5).

You have all the tools you need, with the Bible as your guidebook. Yet, if you still feel yours is a hopeless case, consider the above
Scripture magnifying the covenant that we can stand firmly upon, no
matter how many mistakes we have made. Dig into His Word,
believe and stand on His promises. God is Love! He is faithful and
kind. His character and the good that He wants to do for us really
doesn't depend on what we have or haven't done. He always makes a
way of escape, and surrounds us with His songs of deliverance. He is
always willing to teach us and guide us in our parenting.

*Thou art my hiding place; thou shalt preserve me from
trouble; thou shalt compass me about with songs of deliverance.
Selah. I will instruct thee and teach thee in the way which thou
shalt go: I will guide thee with mine eye* (Ps. 32:7, 8).

3

Cultivating Christian Curriculum

Curriculum is not just something we do each day, but the vehicle that takes our children to their destination. Where do we want them to be when we finish our task? Humanistic curriculum produces an individual who does not need God. He makes his own decisions and runs his own life, according to the way he sees fit. He presents challenges to parents and teachers as a youth and will accomplish little of lasting value as an adult. Although there may be an aura of success and responsibility about this individual, something is seriously lacking. Human gods fail, and this self-god is plagued with underlying disturbances. He cannot meet his own expectations. Life itself does not meet his expectations. Nothing can complete this individual, nothing can create order in his life, nothing can satisfy.

Only God can fill the void in the humanist's life and only a Christian curriculum will result in wholeness for our children. Only if they are drilled, taught and disciplined unto obedience to God, during the strategic years of childhood, will they be at peace with God, themselves and others as an adult. Furthermore, they will live an orderly, habitual and effective way of life. These purposes must be the driving lights of our training and educating. There are other more specific purposes for Christian education:

Christian Classical educators believe that the curriculum should train the child to think and express himself Christianly. The emphasis is on language and reasoning skills which enable the student to fluently defend and promote the Christian faith.

Charlotte Mason was interested in training the will through teaching habits. She also wrote that the child should be fed a rich literary feast, nourishing the mind with lovely and lofty thoughts. An integral part of Miss Mason's teaching was the study of nature. Such studies prompted the child to bow intuitively before the Creator, giving Him praise and glory. Nature study also instilled inquisitiveness about God's world and stimulated learning in all subjects.

Rousas John Rushdoony wrote that Christian education enables the student to discover his aptitudes, so that he can serve God by influencing his area of expertise. Education is not for the student to be:

> . . . *entertained, to "find" himself, realize himself or advance himself, but to know, believe in, obey and better serve the Lord, and be prepared for his calling in the Lord. . . .*
>
> *Christian education thus prepares youth to be priests, prophets and kings in Christ over the world. The prophetic task is to apply God's word to our place in life, our calling, ourselves and our families, to declare and apply God's word. The priestly task is to dedicate ourselves, our calling, homes and tasks to the Lord and His purposes. Our kingly task is to rule ourselves, our homes, callings and jurisdictions in Christ, to exercise dominion in all these areas in the name of the Lord and by means of His law-word. . . .*[1]

➥ Where do you think your child needs to be as an adult? To better choose curriculum that enables progress in learning, skills, wisdom and godliness, compile a list of the ✿ **dreams and goals** you have for your children. Have older children take part in this planning.

CHAPTER 3 CULTIVATING CHRISTIAN CURRICULUM

✗ There is a window of opportunity, open for only a few years. During this time the child is teachable, responsive and pliant. Even if your own lack of childhood training leaves you feeling inadequate, you must not fail with your children. This does not give you license to use the "do as I say, not as I do" philosophy. Instead, pray openly (and privately) in repentance and petition that you might be changed to be the example, all the while teaching diligently and consistently, before the window slams shut.

Heart Training

And thou shalt love the LORD thy God with all thine heart, and with all thy soul, and with all thy might. And these words, which I command thee this day, shall be in thine heart . . . (Deut. 6:5, 6).

The term *heart* refers to the thought life which pours over into the will and flows out through actions. If God permeates the thought life, good will result. The heart is the control center and must be trained to be servant unto God and ruler over flesh. When the child learns to live from his heart for God, educational achievement and high character unfold naturally. Because he desires to please the God he loves and has been trained to obey, he applies himself diligently to the task at hand, with increased productivity in all subjects and pursuits.

The greater result of heart-training is wisdom unto salvation, through faith in Jesus. Moreover, the child will be perfectly equipped for doing good works. His life will have value for God, self and others. It is most assuring to know that ☆ **if the child's heart is molded for God, the Holy Spirit will continue to rule and guide him, even after he is loosed from parental control.**

> **The heart is the control center.**

Education is in vain, if our children do not grow to love and fear God from their hearts. Our most necessary goal, then, is that the heart be trained. A curriculum that teaches otherwise—or even neglects this goal—is not worthy of the Christian homeschooler.

Mrs. Sigourney, mother and a popular and prolific inspirational writer of the mid-1800s said, "The true order of learning should be, first, what is necessary; second, what is useful; and third, what is ornamental. To reverse this arrangement, is like beginning to build at the top of the edifice."

First, What is Necessary

For the word of God is quick, and powerful, and sharper than any two-edged sword, piercing even to the dividing asunder of soul and spirit, and of the joints and marrow, and is a discerner of the thoughts and intents of the heart (Heb. 4:12).

The most effective and only pure curriculum for heart-training is the Word of God. When used liberally, God's Word automatically teaches, rebukes, corrects and trains in righteousness. (2 Tim. 3:16) Some curriculum is tainted with the philosophies of man and dilutes the Word of God, giving your child a mixed message.

Whereby are given unto us exceeding great and precious promises: that by these ye might be partakers of the divine nature, having escaped the corruption that is in the world through lust (2 Pet. 1:4).

The Bible covers each and every area of character training and development and can stand alone as *the* character-building textbook. Particular sections—such as Proverbs—give concentrated doses of necessary wisdom. Some of the best character-building material in the Bible can be found in the biographies of people who lived righteous lives before God and man. Consider Jonah, Noah, King David, Daniel, Paul, Ruth, Esther and numerous others as examples of character to emulate and character to shun.

The Bible is the "Ultimate Life Manual," direct from God. Every word, every chapter, every story, every book tells how to live to please God and have a blessed life. Beyond salvation, this practicality is what I most love about God's Word. It holds the answer for my every question, need and desire. It is perfectly reliable.

The purpose of educating from the Scriptures is not conversion. However, teaching from the Word of God imparts redeeming knowledge, which in turn leads to salvation. We teach; the Holy Spirit saves through the living, God-breathed Word. *Faith cometh by hearing, and hearing by the word of God* (Rom. 10:17).

> The KJV contributes to high SAT scores.

Another benefit of using the Word of God is academic. "The influence of the Bible, particularly the King James version, upon the development of the English language and literature, has been attested to by critics for generations."[2] A student who uses the King James Bible, with its rich vocabulary, will score high in college entrance exams. (The other Bible versions use less specific words and even model incorrect grammar.) The knowledge of God, through knowledge of the Bible, ties all other learning together so that it has meaning and is not merely a collection of facts.

Technique

☆ **The teacher of Scripture must be a student of Scripture**. Learn along with your children but also, in your private devotions, seek to know the Lord and His Word intimately.

Gimmicks, such as project-oriented Sunday school materials, usually deter from the Word, because 1) they rob time from the actual study of the powerful and life-changing Scriptures and 2) they often trivialize God, instead of magnifying Him. *Bible Study Guide for All Ages* includes activities that younger children enjoy, yet this course clearly imparts the most important doctrines of the Word. If you choose to use this activity-based study, continue with a liberal amount of individual and family Bible reading and study.

✔ Along with reading the Bible in a consecutive manner, you can do topical studies. My *Bible Master* software, from The Lockman Foundation, does quick and easy word and verse searches. Other tools are *www.biblegateway.com* and *Nave's Topical Bible*. Choose

a character trait such as *truthfulness* and look up scriptures on truth, liar or lies to find verses on that topic. Another good topic is *the fear of the Lord*. Read the verses, then use selected verses for
❀ **copywork and memory work.** Cover one topic per week.

Rich vocabulary is the result of extensive reading. When a child sees a word in several different places, its meaning is revealed through the context of the sentences. Look up the word if 1) you do not understand it from the context, 2) you need the meaning immediately for an application such as correction or if 3) it is a word used only once in the entire Bible, such as *eschew* or *ensue* (1 Pet. 3:11).

Daily Bible quiet time should be required for all, beginning with a Bible picture book for the toddler. Next, he could do his quiet time with you. You read, and your child follows along in his own Bible. This will give familiarity with the advanced vocabulary of the Authorized (KJV) Version. (See more on Bible training during early childhood in Chapter 5, "Harvesting from History" under topic heading, "The Home and Colonial School Society.")

As soon as the child is able to read fluently, he can read Psalms, Proverbs, Gospel chapters and Bible stories. Chart a path through the Scriptures for younger children. Do not neglect to train this most important life habit. There should be firm consistency. To receive the most benefit, quiet time should include at least one of the following notebook activities.

1) *Bible copywork.* You may assign target scriptures. For instance, if your child needs to obey more fully, find scriptures on obedience.

2) *Bible note-taking.* In the Bible notebook, the child can confess sins, note prayer requests and answers, write special verses and record God's instructions for him. He could use a divided spiral notebook with a section for each of these topics. Use Bible study questions such as the following for the child who does not know how to start.

What is God telling you?
What scriptures did He emphasize to you in your reading?
What does He want you to do?
What sin do you need to confess?

What do you need help with?

What do you want to ask God for?

What do you want to praise God for?

What verse(s) meant most to you?

Perhaps your child does not want you to see these personal notes. You do not have to read them, merely glance to see that quiet time was done each day. (Have your child put the date on each day's notes.)

Other avenues for imparting the Bible's teaching are dictation, rephrasing a passage, researching Bible customs and history, oral or written summations of passages, daily application, family devotions and discussion, speaking the Word, hearing preaching of the Word and going to the Word for situations needing answers.

A teacher and pupil met after twenty years. The pupil said:

Do you remember the commandment you had on the blackboard for a week—"Remember now thy Creator in the days of thy youth?" . . . that marked the beginning of my Christian life, though you never made a comment upon the verse, and you never knew that it was responsible for any change in my life.[3]

✔ Copy a verse from the Bible onto a blackboard or white board or print the verse in a large font and tape it up on the wall. Leave for several days or longer to familiarize your children with the verse and principle. Memorizing will be easy because the child is seeing it continuously.

Second, What is Useful

English social reformer, Edwin Chadwick (1801-1890) said "There is a moral as well as an intellectual objection to the custom, frequent in these times, of making education consist in a mere smattering of twenty different things, instead of in the mastery of five or six."

After Bible, our focus should be on reading, writing and arithmetic. These basic skills should be mastered because they are used throughout life. We cannot be good stewards of the money God gives us, if we do not know math. We cannot read the Scriptures, if we do not know how to read, nor can we learn any other subject. We cannot tell others the Good News, if we are not able to express ourselves understandably.

Math

Basic math functions can be taught simply with ❀ **flash cards**. An inexpensive workbook or a vintage book would work for fundamental concepts. You can teach your older child practical math, such as personal and household accounting. *Saxon Math* is effective because it includes reading, comprehension and drill. If your older student has college goals, they can cover advanced math with self-teaching Saxon.

To teach investing, see *Rich Kid, Smart Kid.* In my experience, investing in God's work not only lays up treasures in heaven but also gives a much better return than traditional investments here and now. (Matt. 6:19, 20)

Reading

We cannot read the Scriptures, if we have not been taught to read. Literacy and high educational achievement are the products of a family life filled with language (speaking, writing and reading). Reading instruction should begin with ❀ **phonics**. The child then needs practice until he reaches reading fluency.

Reading is the most important schooling activity. ☆ **Reading aloud from good books should begin when your child is very young and continue until he leaves your home.** Reading can cover many subject areas. The ☞ **Robinson Curriculum** is an example of a course of study in which every subject, other than math and composition, is taught through reading.

Most pre-1900 literature is moral—if not outright Christian—as is much of what was published up through the 1940s and 1950s. An emphasis on reading well-written materials provides the student with a solid foundation in all subjects, along with high ACT and SAT scores. Literature-learning develops the vocabulary and critical thinking skills required for standardized testing and college entrance exams.

Expression

We cannot share God's Word if we do not know how to express ourselves understandably in speech and writing. These skills flow from reading and will be well done with much early and continued reading. I did not even have to teach spelling to my girls. If necessary, it is best to extract spelling lists from the child's own writing. You may have your child do activities in ❀ **copywork and dictation**. Require penmanship until your child's handwriting is legible and mature.

✔ Along with daily family and school read-aloud sessions, assign classics to your older children and have them do summaries of each book they read. It is best to write each day after that day's reading. Because these summaries focus on well-written literature, your child will learn not only style but also mechanics such as punctuation. I think it is best to say, "Write as much as you can." Otherwise the child may cut off their creativity at the required page or even start doing less than a page. These summaries should be lengthy enough to cover the story line and include some interesting quotes or other notes. Even in non-fiction reports, have your children include something interesting or unusual about the content of the book.

Rushdoony's Suggestions

- *Thought must precede writing. Compositions dealing with ideas are far more useful than, "What I Did on My Vacation." It is far better to deal with "Why Capital Punishment?" and "Should Schools Have Corporal Punishment?"*

- *Copying is good discipline. Students who go to reference books and copy, somewhat altered, materials therefrom, are usually the better students.*

- *Condensing encyclopedia articles is good training. It requires getting to the heart of a matter, seeing essentials and tracing the basic sequence of thought. The teacher can mimeograph magazine and encyclopedia articles and ask all the students to condense the article as a good writing exercise.*

- *Oral composition is excellent training. Talking is composition. . . . Students can be asked to give "How to" talks on their interests, how to bake bread, solder, etc. "How to" writing is also good.*

- *Sentence structure is important. Outlining an essay, locating topic sentences, parsing, etc., all need to be taught.*

- *A proverb from Scripture such as Prov. 13:24 or 28:4, 9, can be used as the first sentence of an essay to develop and explain its meaning.*

- *Children should be assigned words to look up. Then they can write about their history and meaning using the second, unabridged edition of* Webster's, *or the* Oxford Dictionary.

Source: Rushdoony, *The Philosophy of the Christian Curriculum*, p. 52-54.

Training a Writer

1) Read aloud to your young child.
2) Listen to and write down the stories he tells.

If you begin with these two steps, your child will have no lack of creativity in his writing. Even after he is able to write, your child will compose more detailed works if you do the actual writing, at least part of the time. When your child begins writing, be sure all work is completed— and completed neatly. If you accept less, your children will continue to do less than what they are capable of, and may fail to learn important habits, which carry over to other areas, such as dress and cleanliness.

Once your child is writing profusely, the next step is cutting. This step should be saved for later, at about eleven years old or older (depending of course, on your individual child and his writing experience).

Eliminate

- Phrases, sentences or sections not related to the main theme of the writing.
- Groups of words that can be expressed by a single descriptive word.
- High-brow words. Keep it simple.
- Adjectives and adverbs that can be expressed by a descriptive noun or verb.
- Uninteresting details.

After the excess is cut from the writing, the student should make sure the sentences are varied in length and form. Do not use only the subject-verb-object format, but begin some sentences with verb phrases ("Sitting on the shore, he began thinking of his past.") or prepositional phrases ("Amidst the confusion, she was enveloped in a supernatural peace.").

You may also wish to teach the following figures of speech:

- A *simile* expresses comparison using *like* or *as. How like the winter hath thy absence been. So are you to my thoughts as food to life.* (Shakespeare)

- A *metaphor* denotes comparison without the use of like or as. *I am floating in a sea of blessings. Life is a bowl of cherries.*

- *Personification* is the term that describes non-human things as having human qualities or forms. *Flowers danced about the lawn.* In her pioneer novel, *A Lantern In Her Hand,* Bess Streeter Aldrich personified as she penned, *A thousand stars, looking down, paled at its* [the moon's] *rising.*

- *Personified as she penned . . .* in the above sentence is an *alliteration,* meaning that one letter sound is emphasized in a sentence or phrase. Although alliteration makes sentences memorable and adds variety, overuse is extremely annoying. Similes, metaphors, personifications and alliteration can all be overused, but occasional use will add sparkle to writing.

Writing Checklist

❏ Have you used complete sentences?
❏ Do ideas flow from one sentence to the next?
❏ Are the sentences varied in length and type?
❏ Have descriptive words been used?
❏ Have you checked the writing thoroughly?

Editing is correcting, adapting, checking the flow, rewriting, eliminating and adding seasoning. Proofreading is finding and correcting errors, such as missing punctuation or extra spaces. As the student develops his writing skills, these tasks can be done at the same time.

Paragraphs

Paragraphs are a key to organized writing. Each paragraph contains one idea or thought and a topic sentence that sums up that thought in a nutshell. That paragraph also contains supporting sentences that explain or supplement the main idea in the topic sentence. (The first sentence in this paragraph was my topic sentence.)

While writing this book, I found that if I bolded the topic sentences, it was easier to organize my writing. I would then drag (or cut and paste) the supporting sentences to the paragraph with the proper topic sentence. Here is how you could do this with your children:

1) Tell your students to write a rough draft composition (about one or two pages long). Emphasize that their work will be rewritten after they learn a new writing technique. This composition can be about a book read, an experience or trip. It could even be an original story.

2) Next—perhaps the next day—have your children circle, highlight, underline or bold, if using a word processor, the sentences that are most important. These are the topic sentences. In a handwritten one-page essay, there should be approximately two to five.

3) All the supporting sentences need to be gathered together with each topic sentence. A different colored highlighter or pencil could be used for each paragraph. The student highlights or circles the supporting sentences and draws arrows to the circled or highlighted topic sentence.

4) Rewrite into paragraphs, placing each topic sentence with its supporting sentences.

5) Organize the paragraphs by thinking what topic should come first, second and so on.

Other Useful Subjects

It is dangerous and counter-productive to neglect the essentials of learning and clutter the curriculum with social studies, arts, crafts and other courses. Once your child is on his way to proficiency in the basic skills, you may add the following subjects. Most can be studied within the basic framework of reading and reporting (recitation or writing).

Civics. Studies should cover government and law, including Bible law. *God and Government,* a three-book set available from ☞ **Vision Forum**, reinforces submission to God and parents. For elementary economics you may use *Whatever Happened to Penny Candy?*

Cultures. Do not teach the modern humanistic and anti-Biblical concepts of anthropology (the study of man) and psychology (the study of the mind). We should study pagan cultures so we can evangelize, not emulate. (See Chapter 1, "Gathering Flowers," for more on psychiatry.)

Languages. Foreign studies and languages should be geared to reality. Study Spanish to prepare for missionary efforts in the homeland and abroad. The Tacoma, Washington *News Tribune* reported that, because of continuing immigration and a high birth rate among Hispanics, we will continue to see high growth of the use of Spanish in the United States.[4] The web site, *Why Learn a Foreign Language,* reports, "Approximately 17.5 million people (10% of the US population) speak Spanish. By the year 2020, it is predicted that 51 million people will speak Spanish in the US . . . ."[5]

Study Hebrew and Greek to probe into the Bible and Latin to build a foundation for English and the other languages. Charlotte Mason, an Englishwoman, introduced French to her students partly because France was their nearest neighbor. Because we are called to go into all the world and preach the gospel and because we form a world "nation" with all other Christians, perhaps a greater emphasis should be placed on learning conversational languages.

Science. Science for the Christian must center on God as creator and ruler. Otherwise we have modern science, itself a god, whose epitome of success is as creator, with such travesties as cloning and experimentation in other sacred areas.

In science, as in all other subjects, literature builds minds. Carl Weiman, 2002 co-recipient of the Nobel Prize in Physics, although having a natural propensity toward math, tested higher in verbal skills. He read voraciously as a child because his parents did not have a TV. He says this was the best thing they did for his education.[6]

> Study the lives and works of godly scientists.

Godly scientists model humility, because they realize how limited man is and how very little he knows. Respect and love for God spring from a study of His creation in its miraculous and perfect construction. Another important application of science is stewardship, or conservation, which teaches care for God's world. (See *Wild Days* by Karen Kidmore Rackliffe for inspiration and ideas for nature study.)

Science does not equal knowledge or even scholarship. Although God's world and order are infallible, the sciences that examine His world are not. An "exact" science is a misnomer. Too often, science is regarded as having the final word on a subject, when it does not. Too many experiments fail. This ambiguity about science is what I disliked as a high school student and what frustrated me as I taught my young children.

✔ To avoid fragmentation and disorder in science, study the chronological history of scientific discoveries and inventions. It is best to coordinate this with a chronological study of history. Make a ❀ **time line** and put both historical and scientific individuals on it for cohesiveness. Use Bible chronology to study earth science, astronomy, biology and so on. As you read Genesis, study each element as introduced. The "Table of Contents" in the ☞ **Tobin's Lab** catalog will help with the science portion of your ❀ **scope and sequence**, should you wish to base your studies on the six days of creation.

History. The pages of history are filled with heroism, self-sacrifice, love for country and devotion to principle—no matter what the cost. The child who identifies himself with the people of history will be taken out of his smallness and grow into greatness. In studying history, always keep in mind the idea of God's mercy and judgment on men and nations throughout the ages. History reveals the fundamental principle of "sowing and reaping"—also known as "cause and effect," "actions and consequences," "responsibility and rewards" and "sin and punishment." In no other subject area can we see so clearly, by the panorama of man's doings, that the wages of sin is death (Rom. 6:23) and that God's principles never change. For example, the student of history is reminded of the truth that a nation cannot endure when its citizens lack morality. Goldsmith's voice in his "Deserted Village" rings clearly from the past with caution for today:

> *Ill fares the land,*
> *To hastening ills a prey,*
> *Where wealth accumulates,*
> *And men decay.*

World history is rich with heroes, although not always heroes who knew God. Early American history is especially rich with good and great examples of character. Study the Civil War period and the temperance movement. To see American history is to see God working with and for a people, blessing them to be a blessing. To see World War II history and other current history is to see God crushing evil and opening nations for the great end-time harvest. To see current culture is to see God clearly confirming prophecies about the last days.

Third, What is Ornamental

The ornamental sometimes borders the useful, depending on the child's vocation, ministry or career. For example, fine arts training would be useful to an artist but ornamental to a mechanic. Because your child has learned to consistently obey God, and because he has become proficient in the basics and diligent at study, all other subjects chosen will be easily mastered.

When to Begin Educating

We are faced with the opposing philosophies of "better late than early" and "never too early." Tryon Edwards has said, "Fill the bushel with wheat, and you may defy the devil to fill it with tares." Early instruction in truth will best keep out error. Unless you are doing strict "school at home" with your child completing from five to ten workbooks a day, there is little danger of burnout. Be sensitive to your child. If he needs a break, let him go run awhile. Keep standards high and lessons short when he is young, but do not neglect high-quality reading and composition (narration until they are able to write). I do not believe that we should differentiate between boys and girls, lest any child think himself less capable of learning and fail to reach his full potential.

In the Context of Faith

For the Christian homeschool, curriculum is everything done in the context of the parents' Bible-believing faith. The parents bring their world view into every action and subject. Whether you study Christian history (Rushdoony and others), the order of the universe or the order in math, the Bible has the final word. Below are some applications of the Christian curriculum.

Building Character Through Literature

To help overcome our flaws as parents, we can use the lofty examples found in literature. Building character through literature makes the teaching neutral—more apt to be received, especially by the older child, because it is not judgmental or condemning. The literature does the teaching.

> When children see exemplary lives, they are inspired to like character.

The teacher should be the example in her esteem of books. She should read well and interestingly. She should read privately and share from her own books. For reading aloud or for assignments, she can choose character-building selections such as legends, myths, fairy tales, fables, parables, allegories, poetry, short stories and novels.

The loftiest example of great literature, after the Bible, is *Pilgrim's Progress.* Next would be Shakespeare's *Hamlet, Macbeth* and *King Lear.* Even lesser-known or esteemed literature illustrates Biblical principles such as *be not deceived; God is not mocked: for whatsoever a man soweth, that shall he also reap* (Gal. 6:7).

"One of the best discoveries a boy or girl can make is a man or woman of real worth; one who by example has shown the world what the factors are which constitute success and true greatness."[7] Your child will think, "If they could, why can't I?"

We have read rich biographies about Queen Victoria, John Wesley, Charles Spurgeon and Billy Sunday. Sir Walter Scott's life is a powerful example of almost extinct integrity. When Scott's publishing house failed, he refused to file bankruptcy but committed to paying off his debts no matter the cost to him. He worked rigorously to produce many books in a short time, earning what was needed to clear his debts. Clara Barton overcame timidity as a sixteen-year-old teacher by reading her Bible the first day in class and by replacing her shyness with concern for her students. She made it her mission to serve. Frances Willard championed the emancipation of women, but also fought for the purity of home life and temperance. Read about Helen Keller, Booker T. Washington and others. Older students may read Emerson's *Representative Lives,* Carlyle's *Heroes and Hero Worship* and Plutarch's *Lives.* You could search for the books ✎ *Poor Boys Who Became Famous* or *Poor Girls Who Became Famous.*

Fables can teach morals. Which has a more lasting effect— telling your child that lying has consequences and that he shouldn't do it, or the story of the boy who deceitfully cried "Wolf!" over and over and was ignored when he really needed help?

Boys can read *Robinson Crusoe, Around the World in 80 Days, Captains Courageous, Treasure Island* and Cooper's *Red Rover* and *Pilot.* Vintage series books such as *Tom Swift* and the *Pony Rider Boys* also fall in this "good book" category. Books by Horatio Alger and G. A. Henty could be read. Instead of the cheap modern romance, the older girl can read works such as *Lorna Doone, Mill on the Floss, Ramona, The Virginian* or *Princess Aline.* For nature learning choose William J. Long, Frank Owen Payne, Ernest Seton-Thompson and Theodore Roosevelt.

Use poems and short stories. Read "Ernest and the Great Stone Face" by Hawthorne, "Midas and the Golden Touch" and "Vision of Sir Launfal" by Lowell. Sir Launfal starts out in the pride and haughtiness of youth, yet eventually learns that his gift blesses three—the giver, the needy and the Lord.

> *Who gives himself with alms feeds three*
> *Himself, his hungering neighbors and Me.*

✔ Call attention to the elevating themes of literature. Discuss the characters and their actions. List the good and bad traits of the characters. Memorize character-building excerpts. Include recitations as part of each school day.

The above section "Building Character through Literature," is an excerpt from my article by the same name, first published at the Eclectic Homeschool Online site. See *www.eho.org* for the complete article with links to the books mentioned. EHO also features articles, tips and reviews, including a review of my first book, *Easy Homeschooling Techniques.*

Shakespeare

Biblical application was readily apparent when we studied *Macbeth* by Shakespeare. Macbeth listens to witches (evil spirits) and believes their half-truths, which lead him—with his wife's encouragement—to many murders. I asked Ezra and Eli what the lessons were. They contributed "justice will prevail" and "think before you act." We also saw the lesson about the influence of companionship (his wife). Here is the procedure we used in our study:

1) Read Charles and Mary Lambs' version of any play for an overview. I have found stories on the Internet that are not in the newer *Tales from Shakespeare* volumes.

2) Listen to an audio book of the same play. An older video is also an option. I would avoid recent productions from the 1960s to the present because of immodest costuming and frightening special effects.

3) Read the play.

This triple exposure builds familiarity with Shakespeare as well as the particular work you are studying. It is helpful to have individual copies of the text when reading Shakespeare aloud. You could get multiple copies from the Internet or the library.

✔ Another easy idea for getting acquainted with Shakespeare is to find a book of his quotes. Use some of the easier-to-understand passages for copy work, memory work and recitation.

A Potpourri of School Tips

• "In school, as elsewhere, love is a power for good."

• Call attention to "every elevating thought."

• Have a regular recitation each day in character-building: the teacher (or the student) reads or recites a character building poem or story.

• To avoid hopelessness in teacher or student, select only a few governing principles to work on.

• "Treat your pupils with dignified courtesy, always appealing by your actions to their honor. . . . Treat them as though they were noble, and you cause them to become so."

• Never react—think and pray first. Many hurtful words and harmful actions will thus be avoided.

• Have set times for each class, give children a copy of your master schedule and follow it religiously.

• Give rights and privileges, and withdraw them if they have been misused, teaching that bad behavior garners consequences.

• Spelling: "Glance at the word quickly so that you can pronounce it, and then withdraw the eyes from it and write it out. Then compare it with the print and see if the letters correspond exactly. If you have it wrong, write it out two or three times correctly."

• Better to read a few books thoughtfully, than many superficially. The best result of the book is the thought it awakens.

• When coming upon a situation that tends to make us want to quit, we should stop—not to turn back—but to give ourselves time for reflection, prayer and perhaps a new route to our goal.

• Focus on quality, not quantity.

The above tips were quoted or adapted from the 1889 book, *How to Study, A Guide for Pupils' Self Improvement in School and Home* by W. A. Welch A. M. (Chicago: W. M. Welch & Company).

☆ **An hour's bright, wide awake, concentrated, interested study is worth a day's plodding.** This is another reason you should avoid a curriculum such as Abeka video school where the curriculum is in control, not the parent. In these types of programs, the student must complete many hours of work each day. This is often crushing for the child and maddening for the parent who must continually push. If the child gets too many days behind, the company adds even more charges onto their already exorbitant fees. Another problem is that the parents' money is not refundable after a certain time period—the company has a ball and chain around you and your "poor" child for that year. Recently my young adult sons wanted to do something "different," so we undertook this costly and foolish "structured-school" experiment. It must have been so I could warn you!

Giftedness

I believe most of our children have been gifted by God with great intelligence. Homeschooling statistics prove this. We have the opportunity to enhance or demean that gift. With proper tools such as habit, diligence, schedule, Bible, etc., the Christian child—who is highly favored by God—will be a high achiever.

Gifted children are those ". . . who give evidence of high performance capability in areas such as intellectual, creative, artistic, or leadership capacity, or in specific academic fields . . . ."[8]

Gifted children usually exhibit some of the following: creative expression, originality, fluent self-expression, good organizational skills, responsibility, affability, inventiveness, uniqueness, extensive vocabulary, ease of learning, ability to read at an early age, a keen sense of humor, reasoning skills and other similar qualities. Various tests assess giftedness, including IQ testing and the *Stanford-Binet*. Some areas that can be

> If one child in a family is gifted, all the children in that family are usually gifted.

tested are characteristics, verbal, nonverbal, math reasoning, short term memory, creative thinking and critical thinking. If one child in a family is gifted, all the children in that family are usually gifted (within ten IQ points of each other).[9]

All homeschoolers can apply the following ideas to avoid mediocrity and encourage excellence.

- Read aloud, even if your child is capable of reading independently.
- Get to know your gifted child well. Encourage his interests. Give strong support and positive feedback. Gifted children need praise and encouragement.
- Maintain your cool. Gifted children respond better to explanations than brute force.
- Give your child time to tackle new material. Some gifted children may seem to be underachievers in the early years.
- Set high standards. Students thrive on challenge and become stagnant when excellence is not required.
- Help your child recognize that some skills and knowledge are expected for success in day-to-day life. Do not neglect handwriting, math and proper response to authority.
- Work your schedule diligently, yet allow enough time for rest and recreation. A flexible schedule may be in order so that the gifted child can take time to explore certain subjects in depth.
- Be sure your student is kept accountable, so that they do not waste time on trifles. Although enforcing is fully the parent's job, with consistency, the schedule will become self-enforcing.
- Focus on strengths, not weaknesses.
- Allow the child a "say" in planning.
- Allow your child to progress at his own speed.
- Don't give up on your child.
- Be respectful of your child as a person.
- Have reasonable rules and guidelines.
- Accept limitations. Do not push.
- Explore a foreign language, fine or applied arts, music or other areas of interest.

- Some students become weary of school before they are finished. Allow a choice of programs for variety or acceleration, such as options for work-study, early GED testing or advanced placement courses.
- Do not hold your child back. Avoid repetition, memorization or unnecessary work in concepts already known. Rushdoony (*The Philosophy of the Christian Curriculum*) predicted that there would be an acceleration of education— much more would be accomplished in fewer years. Keeping the student in school for years—"just because"—is detrimental. The student sometimes feels that he is wasting his time and does not do as well as previously.

✔ Vary your techniques from questions to retelling, from written to oral work. Make suggestions. Help your pupils discover the joy of finding the golden nuggets of the subject. Discussion develops thought. Never allow unnecessary distractions during school. The child needs to develop focus. Looking at books or doodling deters from this aim. Encourage note-taking. Have your children come to class with notebooks in order to write down assignments, the teacher's suggestions and selected Bible verses to look up in their quiet time, as well as important points about what was covered.

4

Drawing from my Diary
A Portrait of Our School
1996 (Ages 9—13)—2002 (Ages 15—19)

*A*fter beginning with the grandest hopes and sweetest dreams, the journey has become wearisome. The labors of parenting and teaching are heavy on your mind.

A respite is in order. Refresh yourself with a cool drink from the spring and take a look at my journal. Perhaps you will find some ideas to use in your own homeschool. Marva Collins said, "Anything works, if the teacher works." With homeschooling, anything works if you are involved with your children in a consistent manner.

It was difficult for me to begin work on this chapter because I miss my young children, so pliable and willing to learn. Do not, I beg of you, neglect those special years with your children. They pass by much too quickly.

Fall 1996

September. We took our hymnals out to the big front porch and began a beautiful day with praise. Ezra, ten, chose a Bible chapter to read, which just "happens" to be the keystone of our faith (John 19). Later, Ezra and Jessica, thirteen, looked up verses on . . . *the sin which doth so easily beset* . . . (Heb. 12:1). Ezra copied his, while

Jessie memorized and recited hers. Yes, it did help change the atmosphere! We have been:

- Listening to Bible teaching tapes.
- Reading a biography of a man of faith.
- Doing oral grammar (Abeka).
- Finishing a *Learning Language Arts through Literature* book.
- Learning to sing melody and harmony of some beautiful old hymns.

We purchased *Math Blaster* and *Rosetta Stone.* I believe they offer scant education for the time spent, but the kids are anxious to use them and are motivated to get their other work done first. We began listening to the Bible on tape, dramatized by Shakespearean actors. After working with *Math Blaster,* Eli said that flash cards and *Calculadder* are faster.

✗ When you give your kids a break for recess, go outside too. To reduce stress, find something physical to do, such as riding a bike as fast as you can, up and down the street.

Winter 1996-1997

December. We are reading Charles Dickens' book, *David Copperfield,* which contains autobiographical portions. (This title was his personal favorite.) We viewed a charming old video of his *Christmas Carol.* Then, while on a Christmas lamplight walk through the authentically restored homes and shops of our living museum, we found an attractive Dover unabridged copy of this book. We are learning a carol from the "Christmas Harmonies" tape from ☞ **The Lester Family.**

January. Much more is getting done since we began diligently working a schedule. The boys are improving and are beginning to enjoy the consistency. The girls love it; they like to see their schedule spaces filled out, indicating a day of accomplishment.

✔ Print out ❀ **blank schedules** for each of your children. As your children complete their work, let them fill in what they did that day. Jessica prefers her big desk calendar.

February. We read of the atrocities during the Russian and French revolutions. We are also studying the Rapture and the Great Tribulation (1 Thess. 4:14-5:11; Rev. 3:10,11; Matt. 26) and the "oil" in the virgins' lamps (Matt. 25). Oil lubricates, supplies, covers, polishes, protects. A good discussion question is, "What does the oil represent?"

Spring 1997

March. Today we read—dramatically—the dialogue of an old primary health text. We all laughed as nine-year-old Eli played Dad and deepened his voice accordingly. We are also beginning the vintage book, *Boy Scouts with the Allies in France.* It is about World War I, which is the period of history we are now studying. Another old book, *The Great Answer,* is packed with testimonies of God's mighty protecting hand during World War II. *Sergeant York and the Great War* is available from ☞ **Mantle Ministries** or ☞ **Vision Forum.**

May. We still have a few lessons to finish up. Would like to continue with Bible class and reading aloud each day before we go off to our summer projects. There are just too many good books to read, such as *What Ever Happened To Justice?* I would love to buy one for every magistrate in the USA.

Summer 1997

June. We prepared and ate breakfast on the patio, then worked hard together. The boys helped their dad tear down a shed. Zephi and I scraped the garage in preparation for painting and Jessica kept the kitchen clean. There's no fun like work!

Have been reading the magnificent *America's God and Country*. I can't say enough about this book of quotes by our founders and other important Americans. This work proves, without a doubt, that America's foundation is Christian.

July. Yesterday the boys sang "the baby-sitting blues" when they first awoke, teasing Jessica and Zephi about changing dirty diapers at their new job. Today I sat on our porch swing and watched the girls go to orientation. Oh, how much easier to let them go at thirteen and fourteen, than at five and six! It also helps to know they are only two houses away.

> They stepped off our pillared porch onto the walk, crossed the street, passed the neighbor's picket fence and turned up the sidewalk.

I prepared our ❀ **scope and sequence** to submit to the state. We will study American government, modern history and current events. Other components of our plan:

- *Wordsmith Craftsman* for the girls
- English and American prose and poetry
- A few international classics
- *Saxon* or one of our vintage math texts for the boys

August. We are ❀ **keeping credits** for the girls' high school records. After viewing a creation video about the Glen Rose, Texas, excavations, where dinosaur and human footprints were found together, the girls recorded 1.5 actual hours for science. Watched the *The Spirit of St. Louis* last night. Then we read an eyewitness account of the 1927 mobbing after Lindberg landed in Paris. (History—2.5 hours.) We are also going to include the girls' baby-sitting hours from their summer job for Home Economics.

Visited Ashfall fossil beds in northeastern Nebraska. We couldn't agree with their theory that volcanic ash killed the rhinos, three-toed horses and other animals in the mud hole. It seemed more like remains from Noah's Flood. Additionally, their evolutionary exhibit clearly disproved the link between those horses and today's horses, rather than authenticating it.

Fall 1997

September. I love reading aloud with my children near me. The possibilities for materials are endless, and many are free. Follow these steps for literary learning.

1) First create your ❀ **plan**. This is important.

2) Start with a topic or an individual.

3) Choose children's books from the library on that topic. You may also choose books from the adult section.

4) Take your books home and cuddle in. This activity is ideal for winter, especially if it is snowing. One warm day we read on our porch, with rain falling all around us. Be prepared. Have those books at home before the blizzard or rain starts.

5) Collect classics for your own library.

6) Saturate your children with one topic by reading for hours and hours, days and days.

7) Then, on another day, soon after your reading blitz, supervise the creation of reports, essays, projects, artwork and experiments relating to the topic or person studied. ☞ **Kids Art** sells inexpensive project guides.

October. I am convinced that the secret to success in the basics is consistency. For precept must be upon precept, precept upon precept; line *upon line, line upon line; here a little, and there a little . . .* (Is. 28:10).

✔ If you are not doing it, form the habit of school every day, at least Monday through Friday. Your efforts will be multiplied. The next habit to form would be to begin each school day at the same reasonably early hour. Fresh and rested, in an atmosphere of warmth and consistency, your children will come to the feast of learning with receptive hearts and minds.

The boys are improving in spelling and writing. I have them write every day. If not a summary of Dickens' *Child's History of England,* then a book report. Sometimes I dictate from *Learning Language Arts Through Literature*. Get a like-new copy from ☞ **Second Harvest**. This week, the girls were given independent research assignments, and together we studied "The Fear of the Lord," looking up the scriptures in a topical Bible (*Naves*). We are also going through *Biology Experiments for Children*.

November. Gave the boys a spelling test. Ezra jumped three grade levels in six weeks. I attribute it to increased writing—including from dictation. We use poems or short passages from classics. He then learns the words he misspells.

Winter 1997-1998

December. The boys have started a ☞ **Contenders for the Faith** club with their dad. They are building models of masted sailing ships, and are learning the name of each tiny part. You could create your own club for boys or girls.

• Decide what you want to learn.
• Use a topical Bible to find related scriptures.
• Find books from the library on these topics.
• Have your children read, report, do.
• You could create badges for each topic.

The children put on a Christmas performance for us. Zephi designed and made the programs. Each child read a carol story and played the piano. Ezra, twelve, read the Christmas story from Luke, ending so appropriately with Jesus' temple experience when he was twelve years of age.

January. We are reading a book about Billy Sunday (❀ **excerpt**) written while he was working as an evangelist. What joy to read his simple, and sometimes humorous, way with words. This treasure of a book has photographs of Sunday, his family and the wooden tabernacles that were constructed for each meeting. Modern biographies fall far short in holding interest and exemplifying fine English.

We began reading an article in *American Heritage* (Vol. 30, No. 5) about the mastodon skeleton that Charles Willson Peale unearthed for his museum. Peale was a famous Revolutionary Period painter, having painted the scene, "Exhumation of the Mastodon." We read of it first in *All about . . . Strange Beasts of the Past.* The primary goal of Peale's museum was "To diffuse a knowledge of the wonderful works of creation." I thought it interesting that his sons were named after famous painters: Titian, Rembrandt, Reubens, and Raphael. Even Titian II, his grandson, was an artist.

> Tennyson's poems are airiness and solitude in a warm meadow, the drone of a bee on a flower, a gurgling brook nearby.

February. Henry Wadsworth Longfellow—the people's poet—expressed emotions for the common man. He was called ". . . the poet of the young and pure in heart." His "Evangeline" has lovely descriptions of place and a strong story line. We have been reading a few of his poems each day and yesterday Eli wrote his own poem:

The Son is shining,
The Son is shining,
Deep down in my soul;

The devil is running,
The devil is running,
As fast as he may go;

And I am singing,
I am singing,
To this very day;

To the Lord of Hosts,
Who made this very day.

Spring 1998

March. Alfred Lord Tennyson wrote of nature and love. Unlike Tennyson, Longfellow carried an undercurrent of sadness throughout many of his poems. They also seem to be less refined. Our next poet is Browning.

> Ah . . . sweet poetry!

We are reading "As You Like It" from Lambs' *Tales from Shakespeare,* since we found that video at the library. It seems to me that the gorgeous costumes and settings distract from the dialogue. Audio tapes would keep the creative switches on in the brain and yet help in comprehension since the lines are read dramatically.

Yesterday we completed Lambs' "Merchant of Venice." So far, I think that there is "much ado about nothing" with Shakespeare. Sure, some phrasing is lovely, but the stories seem so flippant, like Andy said, "a soap opera." Maybe we are missing deeper meanings that come from deeper study, or perhaps our choices are wrong. But the end of "Merchant . . ." even included joking about sin. I didn't like the prejudice against Jews and against Shylock in particular, even though he seemed to be a wicked scoundrel. Could the bias of the world, and especially of Germany of the 1940s, have come partly from Shakespeare's widely read writings?

April. Eli, ten, narrated "The Pied Piper" by Robert Browning with much detail. The children described Browning in one word— love. Browning's poems, and his biography (*British Authors of the Nineteenth Century* by Kunitz and Haycraft) confirmed that Browning had an exuberant personality. He loved life and people. His poems ring with a positive note, even when touching on potentially negative concepts.

Narration improves mental capacity and speaking abilities. Now instead of "Well, you see," "that's about all," and "this guy," the children are listening more carefully and thinking before they speak.

Today we read chapter twenty of *Ivanhoe* as well as Shakespeare's "Merchant . . ." (the play, in the original language).

We are understanding it more because we saw the video. Fifteen-year-old Jessica enjoyed the humor of Scene II. Seeing the video—becoming familiar with the story line—helped me read dramatically. I am beginning to like Shakespeare. I can certainly identify with such themes as ". . . I can easier teach twenty what were good to be done, than be one of the twenty to follow mine own teaching. . . ."

Summer 1998

June. Ezra is finishing his *Saxon 54* book. I was able to get an extra *Saxon 65* so that each of the boys could have their own books. They will be able to do math early in the morning, after quiet time, as they prefer. A high quality alternative to *Saxon* books are vintage math texts or reprints, such as the *Practical Arithmetics* series.

Through internet homeschooling groups, such as those at *www.yahoogroups.com,* we were able to sell over two hundred dollars worth of used personal homeschooling materials. We then purchased the ☞ **Robinson CDs.** (❀ **review**) I am impressed with the Robinson Method's high-quality vintage books and simple—yet literary—method of learning. No, you don't need to spend a lot of money to give your children a quality education but, as I have said elsewhere, we spend because we choose to. Since God provided, I chose to purchase.

✔ There are less expensive ways to do Robinson-style homeschool today. ☞ **Home School Treasures**

July. Eli is doing two lessons a day in *Saxon 54.* Ezra is reading *Try and Trust* by Horatio Alger and Zephi is comparing two old books, *The School Queens* by Mrs. L.T. Meade, and *Phil the Fiddler* by Alger. Jessica recently finished a detailed report on the *The Scarlet Pimpernel.* She is reading *In the Reign of Terror* by G. A. Henty (see "Reaping from Reviews," Chapter 7). I have been staying up late to read a vintage book by Mrs. Meade. It models strong sibling loyalty, love in marriage and open prayer.

August. Since the weather has cooled, my thoughts again turn to school and the quantity of reading I want each child to do per day. I am interested in helping them "sink their teeth" into some really great books.

Fall 1998

September. Jessica, fifteen, excitedly told me she discovered an interesting geography title on our bookshelf. It was a Van Loon. She went on to describe it, telling of his suggestions for drawing maps. She is looking forward to starting school and has done planning and scheduling.

I am writing this in the wee hours of the morning. It was 101 degrees today, but now is quite cool. Katydids are singing. A moment ago I heard an owl's tremulous wailing, sounding like an Indian at our back door!

We are going to experiment with Dr. Robinson's ideas for awhile, but not necessarily all the same books. His plan is to do math first, then a one page essay, then read, read, read for a total schooling time of about five hours, with a two hour minimum of reading.

School orientation today! I told the children the simple "one, two, three" of it and they said, "That's all?" They are all up working quietly in their rooms now and it is only about 8:00 a.m. The boys have math done. Eli had been a long way from finishing *Saxon 54,* yet, according to the placement test, is able to start *76.* We decided to go with *65,* test mid-year and advance him at that time.

✔ Do not hold your child back! Success and advancement will breed more success.

> **We brought all the fish home, save one.**
> *Ezra Curry*

Ezra wrote about going fishing with his dad the previous night. Eli's essay was titled "The Outhouse Atop the Hill." Although they are studying more independently, I interact as I correct daily essays and math, discuss the books and essays and print vocabulary drill sheets. Andy reads the children's essays after our evening meal.

✔ Keep your kids close if you use a self-teaching method such as Robinson. Schedule in reading aloud and other family times. There is a tendency to neglect interaction.

October. Zephi checked out a two-foot stack of Robinson books including a facsimile copy of a Conan Doyle and *The Complete Uncle Remus.* Eli got a good start on an Alger book today. The boys wrote their essays on the country home we looked at—on top of a high hill with twenty-six acres of hilly pasture and lots of animals in barns and sheds.

November. Last night I began reading aloud from Louisa May Alcott's *An Old Fashioned Thanksgiving.* This is published by Applewood Books and available from ☞ **Home School Treasures**

We attended a free recital and reception for The American Chamber Players at the Museum of Nebraska Art. Jessica heard of it on Nebraska Public Radio. The music was lovely; the building—an old post office—was impressive with its polished marble floors and expansive ceilings. We also enjoyed "A Nebraska Sketchbook," by Mary Louise Tejeda, a transplanted Californian, whose Mexican father and Swiss mother had moved from Mexico City to avoid the violence of the revolution there. This artist lives in the western part of our state, and used pastels to catch the quickly changing colors of Nebraska's lovely unspoiled scenery.

Winter 1998-1999

January. Jessica's handwriting has matured into a unique style. She started with cursive, went to italic and then back to cursive. Ezra has made progress this year in spelling because silent reading is a larger part of our curriculum. I suggested that he pay closer attention to spelling when he reads. That has helped. They are producing creative and humorous stories. Zephi has had no problems with math and seems to race through her reading, having finished more books than any of the others this year.

February. Eli wrote on sugaring. We have one huge maple tree that I had always thought of tapping. The boys are doing it. They gathered over three gallons of sap one warm day and later made syrup. They found how-to information in *Countryside* magazine, encyclopedias and in *The Encyclopedia of Country Living.*

We read aloud from Dr. Dabney's *Stonewall Jackson.* I loved his definition of true courage (see Chapter 7). Jessica wrote a paper on ✍ *Of the Motion of the Heart and Blood in Animals* by William Harvey who lived in the 1600s. Another day she copied from this extremely well-written book.

Spring 1999

March. I read aloud from Foxe's *Book of Martyrs.* Eli is reading Conan Doyle's *Stories for Boys.* The girls have a two-week babysitting job, so the boys and I began a vintage biography of Charles Spurgeon. He was sixteen when he started preaching and after only a few years was ministering to huge crowds in London. The first part of the book is biography, the second, sermons.

April. Eli started ✍ *The Rover Boys on Treasure Isle* by Arthur Winfield after finishing *Swiss Family Robinson.* I purchased *Key to Algebra* for Jessica. Some say that *Key to Algebra* is best done before *Saxon Algebra.* Perhaps this is why Zephi is not having any trouble with *Algebra I*—she did *Key to Algebra* last year. The children have been reading silently two to three hours a day, but I missed our reading together. There are so many great books on our shelves that I want to share. Along with the book on Spurgeon, we are finishing a book about people of God from the early 1900s. What a special experience to see the Holy Spirit minister here, now, today, through words spoken from the past. Our reading yesterday included applications for young people—perfect for our own young adults who now not only listen, but contribute.

May. Jessica cleaned the yard last week and did a terrific job. Today the six of us sat on the patio in the beautiful warm air and read from the Bible and the ✍ *Royal Path of Life.* Ezra has read a book a day for the last three days. He also finished his math book. Hurrah!

We are reading one of our "finds," ✍ *Two Little Savages,* by Ernest Seton-Thompson. The boys beg me to read more and have done excellent narrations of it. Eli and Zephi both finished their math books. We have been drilling Bible verses (Heb. 11:13, Ps. 119:1-8).

✔ First we read the verse many times in unison, next we recite it together many times, and then the children recite individually as much as they know of it. I also suggested that they study it during their quiet times.

Eli just brought me some of his work—he did it before going to sleep. He started his new *Saxon 76* today and I was excited to see a neat paper with no errors. He is also finishing his italic handwriting workbook. He is doing cursive italic and I see improvement. Even his copywork is neater. He has been copying the same scriptures for about three days and the one he just did certainly looks better than the first, or even the second. Moreover, I am sure he has learned them by heart after three days of doing the same verses.

Spring 2000

January. I asked the children to tell me some of their goals for that week, for school and for their lives, as I wrote them down. On Friday, most of the week's goals had been accomplished without any prodding on my part. I also made my own lists for each of the children. On Friday I began filling in assignment books—Day Runners®—that I had found on clearance. First I chose a stack of books for each child. Then I listed the actual pages that Ezra and Eli needed to cover each day. Instead of one-fifth of her book, Jessica read the entire book and wrote about it for her daily two-page essay. Zephi's writing was the best she had ever done—a flowery description of the view from her upstairs window. (If you continue with high quality books, you *will* see improvement.)

May. Our children have finished their math books and have the following summer school requirements.

- Read Bible
- Copy one Bible chapter.
- Read one-fifth of a selected book per day.
- Write a one-page report on that book.
- Continue in ☞ *Simply Spelling* (Ezra and Eli).

Eli is reading *Tom Sawyer;* Ezra, *The Spirit of St. Louis;* Jessica, *Autobiography* by Theodore Roosevelt. Zephi says that she is going to complete the Robinson book list this summer.

June. We have been digging thistles at our country property. Musk thistles can grow to over five feet tall and have a large soft purple flower. The former owner told us he had introduced weevils to feed upon the thistle seeds to help control them, and sure enough, we saw them at work when we broke open the flowers. Musk thistles are called "bull" thistles in *Spotters Handbook* which is a favorite, although out-of-print, nature guide. It has simple color artwork of the most common trees, flowers and birds of North America. Another day, I saw several American Goldfinches bathing in the brook, then landing on tall thistles to pull out the seeds (or the weevils). I was thankful I had binoculars. It was like watching a nature movie! That day we also saw and identified a Cedar Waxwing.

August. I am enjoying Jessica, seventeen, more than I ever have. I really missed her sunshine personality when she was working so much this summer. She recently took practice ACT and SAT tests. One afternoon we added up actual hours to compute ❀ **credit hours**. We also averaged grades for her transcript. (A transcript must include the date that the student left school and their date of birth.) Jessica kept great records! We wrapped the calculator tape—just for 9th grade—around Dad three to four times. It encouraged us all to realize that we actually did accomplish something.

Fall 2000

September. "School days, school days, Oh, those golden rule days." My dad used to sing this old tune to awaken me each morning. Although he may have meant well, it aggravated me because I hated school. That is why I'm here. I would never trade this lifestyle for any other. I am determined to make the best of the time I have left with my young adults who are thirteen, fifteen, sixteen and almost eighteen. I will be the first to admit that we need Holy Spirit-led school. Without the Holy Spirit to direct and enable us, we could do nothing.

October. We can have the best ❀ **schedule** on paper, but if a habit is not formed to keep that schedule, our planning is in vain. We have had over a month of schedule-keeping now, and I intend to keep it up. One of our classes is Speech. Speech skills are so important. We are striving for the most important qualities of speech including clear, controlled and varied voices. It is helpful to tape speech practice and critique each speaker.

November. Students can learn science—simply—from books. Beyond details is the wonder of the discoveries. *O LORD how manifold are thy works! in wisdom hast thou made them all: the earth is full of thy riches* (Ps. 104:24). We are reading *Madame Curie,* the excellent biography (by daughter Eve) of Marie Curie, co-discoverer of polonium and radium.

✔ Our four have memorized Prov. 5:1-14, a good "warning" for young adults. We are also learning other Bible passages. Have your children copy a Bible passage each day for several days, then dictate. Next, test memorization. Finally, begin recitations. Recitation was the primary learning tool of the past (see more in Chapter 6, "Raising the Standard").

Winter 2000-2001

December. Jessica completed her high school graduation and Bible college entrance requirements. She will be leaving right after Christmas. The Lord has loosed angels to pave the way for this momentous and life-forming move of God in her life. *It takes a village.* I can see God's original concept in action here. Members of our big faith family have upheld her and pushed her through God's open doors. Special people prayed, some daily, that nothing would interfere with God's plan for her life. It was difficult to let go of our our dear eldest daughter, since homeschooling has allowed our family to become so close.

> I can finally identify with Hannah!
> *(1 Sam. 1:22)*

However, God prepared me to untie the apron strings by a series of events that turned me totally around. I now know that her departure is the right thing—the only thing. We now willingly sow the finances and our firstfruits—our firstborn— back to Him for his use and glory. I can *finally* identify with Hannah.

Jessica took the ACT test again last Saturday. She used the *Kaplan Emergency Prep: SAT, ACT* from the library for cramming. In your school, be sure to cover all of the basic areas of study— writing, reading, social studies, history, math and science. Homeschoolers seem to do better on the literary areas of college entrance tests, and not as well on the math and science portions. These tests measure comprehension more than knowledge, which is a plus for most homeschoolers. Comprehension is enhanced by having a full vocabulary, and vocabulary is enhanced by using the King James Bible throughout the years of homeschooling. More science in high school is also a good idea, especially if you have not done much previously. Algebra is the focus of the math portions of the tests. Students are allowed to use a math calculator. You can cover algebra and geometry by using Saxon. Calculus and physics will help your child achieve high scores on the ACT and SAT.

My primary goal for our children is that they grow into fine young Christian adults, not that they succeed academically, although that, too, is almost guaranteed with home-schooling. With this first step into life with our first child, we are beginning to realize

> Homeschooling holds eternal weight.

our goal. Even if your child is not a stellar student, even if you have not had the ideal homeschool, you have had the opportunity to be with your child each and every day of their youth and that will have eternal weight.

January. I have no greater joy than to hear that my children walk in truth (3 John 1:4). No greater joy. I was rejoicing at Jessica's decision to go to Bible college and remembered this scripture. That's the bottom line. Not scholarship, not awards, but that our children walk in truth. Jessica left on December 29th and is now in Columbus, Ohio—away from home for the first time ever. Do our responsibilities stop here? No. The biggest responsibility is to lift her to the throne of God regularly as she learns to make right decisions on her own. I sent her the following "suggestions."

Ten College Commandments

1) *Have faith in God.* Do not depend on any person. This is a heart matter.

2) *Stay out of money trouble.* Do not borrow, use credit or spend more than you have budgeted.

3) *Keep your eyes on the goal.* Do not be distracted. Keep your eyes on Jesus. Keep focused on seeking His will.

4) *Eat healthfully.*

5) *Get proper sleep.* With a rigorous schedule of classes and work, you will need your sleep for optimal health.

6) *Trust God, not man.* Do not trust anyone too much, even your closest acquaintances.

7) *Keep clean.* Just because your parents are not supervising you, don't forget God sees all. *Neither is there any creature that is not manifest in his sight: but all things are naked and opened unto the eyes of him with whom we have to do* (Heb. 4:13).

8) *Avoid close relationships with opposite sex.* Do not become too close to any boys or men; let your best friends be girls.

9) *Wait on the Lord.* There are a lot of fish in the sea and you will see an enormous beautiful ocean there, but wait on the Lord for the perfect catch, should that be His will for your life.

10) *Pray for those at home.* Remember us here who are praying for you daily and wanting God's best for you.

February. While Zephi schools independently, Ezra, Eli and I have been reading aloud about interesting events in the lives of the presidents, which took us to Thomas Jefferson, the writer of the Declaration of Independence. We read the Declaration, discussed it, and they wrote a summary of Jefferson's biographical information. We then read Washington's inaugural address. I was thrilled at the similarities between it and President Bush's inaugural speech, regarding individual responsibility and the honor shown to God. However, the writing style has changed greatly. Washington's sentences were long and complex with advanced vocabulary; Bush's, short and fragmented. Zephi is graduating in March or April. She has finished most subjects, but is working on her Graduation speech. She liked President George W. Bush's speech, and will be studying other presidents' inaugural addresses.

Jessica's favorite subject is "Intro to Christian Education." "It has the most and hardest assignments but I'm never bored . . . ." She is also taking "New Testament Literature," "Introduction to Evangelism," "Spiritual Warfare" and "Bible Study Methods."

Spring 2001

March. Ezra, Eli and I read, copied and discussed "To-morrow" by Samuel Johnson on procrastination. We looked up unfamiliar words and couldn't find one, even in our 1800s dictionary. We decided it was probably misspelled, or that the spelling had changed. Ezra, fifteen, formerly a reluctant writer, is writing a historical 1840s fiction piece. His interests focus on the skills of that time. He spends his free time on projects like making knives and candles and reading non-fiction books on these topics. Ezra and Eli, thirteen, have nearly the same schedule. They do their independent work from about 6:00 to 10:00. This includes *Saxon Algebra 1/2* (Eli, *Saxon 87*), reading from classic and vintage books, penmanship practice and writing. From 10:00 a.m to 12:00 noon we read together from the Bible and a vintage biography, classic novel or other book. After this, they often write or narrate.

One of the classics we read together is *Great Expectations*. Christian study guides for this book and others are available from Dr. Robert Watson. **www.smarrpublishers.com**

April. Zephi received the scores from her first ACT test. The composite score was seven points above her sister's first test score, and two points above Jessica's second score. It was surprising that she scored higher in science than in some other test areas. Science was definitely not emphasized in our school. In Zephi's case, her advanced math courses may have helped. We are planning her graduation for April 28th. We have ordered her class ring from Israel. It is sterling silver with her name cut out in Hebrew letters. Zephi is mostly self-educated, having taught herself to read at age five by sitting in on her sister's phonics classes and finishing up her last several years of school entirely on her own.

> We ordered Zephi's class ring from Israel.

The boys and I have been reading Shakespeare. Shakespeare is stretching us all, but stretching is necessary for growth and learning. While the story line is not difficult to follow, the vocabulary is challenging, presenting an opportunity for vocabulary study.

1) Look up selected words.

2) Write in a notebook.

3) Review.

> Yes, we can keep it simple and still achieve much with our children.

May. We are continuing with reading and narrations. Zephi spent hours on her graduation speech after she finished school, proving that life is school and that learning does not stop when our children graduate. I was pleased to look once again through her essay notebooks, full of varied and good writings—although neither perfectly neat nor error-free.

Summer 2001

Unless a child is involved in numerous self-directed and outside interests, the best activity for that child may be to continue with schooling in the summer. I plan to continue reading aloud and working on some skills with Ezra and Eli. Narration will cover rhetorical skills, while reading aloud, reading silently and writing will cover spelling and grammar.

Colleges take a close look at standardized test scores when weighing homeschool applications and find that homeschoolers outperform their school-educated peers. In a recent year, homeschoolers scored an average of 1,100 on the SAT—a full 81 points above the national average—and 22.8 on the ACT, compared with the national average of 21. Zephi's "EasyHomeschooling" score of 27 qualifies her for selective admissions colleges.

July. And what have we been learning lately?

Construction—Ezra, Eli and I have begun to remodel the bathroom. We are tearing out plaster, lathe, blown-in insulation, windows and rebuilding walls. Our sons are learning how to prioritize. Work must precede pleasure and their most recent "pleasure" is . . .

Small engine mechanics—Eli got a great deal on a used riding mower when he told the young man it was his birthday. Our neighbor gave Ezra a mower, and now several of their friends have them too. Ezra and Eli have been helping the others get their mowers running.

August. Zephi is looking for a job so she can save for college. She helps me with dishes, laundry and cleaning. The rest of her time is spent taking care of her many animals and sewing. Ezra and Eli have been cleaning the basement and the workshop, and working for others. Eli, fourteen, has earned money by fixing a mower, mowing lawns and—with Ezra, fifteen—doing light construction work.

Fall 2001

September. We have so much going on now in "real life." We are still not even half done with our "do-it-yourself" remodeling, so school hasn't started yet, but I have been preparing by praying. The potential plan is "more required." As I choose vintage books from my shelves, I find that I am looking forward to sharing deep truths and interesting facts with the boys. They have had shop classes this summer with our remodeling project. Ezra has been studying electricity for years and did our wiring. Eli worked on plumbing.

November. There has been too much flexibility in our schedule. My own lack of discipline has not helped. Most days, at the very least, I have felt defeated, but as I determined that homeschooling was a binding commitment, I have determined that I will not let my sons grow up unlearned and unholy. Determination is so very important. When we keep on keeping on, even if weary in well-doing, we can be sure we will reap.

Winter 2001-2002

December. It is dark, cold, rainy and windy—and it's late. Do I hear a motor? I look out the window and see Orville and Wilber Wright pushing their prototype flying machine back into the shed. No, wait! It's the Curry brothers who, in two days, created a go-cart out of two riding mowers. Okay, maybe they still need educating, but they are talented and creative. I have seen these machines in stores. They cost thousands of dollars. Won't their younger friends be surprised when they see what they have done? The best part is that they worked together well and peacefully.

Spring 2002

April. It is almost nightfall and Ezra, sixteen, isn't back yet—he went to the river alone to check his traps. I think of his trapping and the coyote he wants to get. Yesterday he skinned a large "grand-daddy" road-kill raccoon. He plans to hang the fur on his wall. Our oldest son is an introvert, often preferring quietness and solitude. He is gifted in math but lost interest in Algebra this year. Being a practical person, he thinks he will never use it. I really don't have any answers—other than to tell him to do it in faith because he may need it someday. Tonight he got a rabbit and used it to re-bait his trap.

Eli, fourteen, is always ready to help his dad or any one of the neighbors. He does all kinds of jobs, sometimes for pay and some-times not. He is a great negotiator and can talk both children and adults into paying him what he thinks he deserves. He has an interest in and talent for mechanical work. He also has an imagina-tive mind and writes engaging compositions.

Ezra and Eli are working together two days a week for a farmer, clearing his pastures of small cedar trees. They are so much more mature than I was, even in my twenties. They know much more about many things and work more than I ever did at home. They are the first to volunteer and have chosen to spend many hours doing community service. They even attended a Village Board meeting with friends. I am thankful that God has allowed Ezra and Eli to develop unique talents through homeschooling.

May. It was a bright day, nearly hot. When I arrived in the country with my bag of books there were big fluffy rain clouds gathering. Yet as I sat there sketching, I looked up and the clouds were gone! I thanked the Lord for doing that just for me. I sat on a quilt on the hill covered with native grass, right where we plan to move our 1907 house, and sketched. Then I read *Pocketful of Pinecones* and later wrote in the hushed surroundings. It was nearing sunset when I took a walk near the creek. A wild duck couple cruised overhead. A bird called for its mate and the turkeys made their familiar sound as they bedded down for the night in the woods below our site on the cliff. I packed up my belongings, followed the golden sun-globe westward toward home, refreshed and renewed.

June. Pau Hana—"I'm finished with my work" (Hawaiian). As my children become more independent, I naturally become less necessary in their lives. I'm not finished yet, but the day is nearing and I'm at peace with it. What is praiseworthy is that the Lord has brought me to this point. It seems such a very short time ago that I found their departure from home far too painful to ponder. God knows just how to bring us to the place of release in our lives. He's done it miraculously with me, and He will do it for you. However, the job will never be completely over for any Christian mother. Believing prayer increasingly supplants direct intervention.

> I packed up my belongings, followed the golden sun-globe westward toward home, refreshed and renewed.

✘ Begin your own heirloom diary. Make your diary unique. Instead of just recording school activities, include special thoughts about each child's strengths and prayers regarding weaknesses. Include God's answers—their growth in knowledge and character. Who knows? Someday you may wish to publish your diary, at least for your own children and grandchildren.

5

Harvesting from History

The thing that hath been, it is that which shall be; and that which is done is that which shall be done: and there is no new thing under the sun (Eccl. 1:9).

I am convinced that the best days of mankind—and the best days of education—have passed. We are bombarded by distractions, while pure, simple and effective education falls by the wayside. We are overwhelmed with curriculum and lifestyle choices—many of which only lead us to squander valuable time while sure educational methods are neglected. What to do? Take the narrow road and stay with the old ways. Study historical educators and their methods to connect with rich ideology. Separate the wheat from the chaff and then travel your own schooling road the richer for having paused to look toward the past.

In *Easy Homeschooling Techniques* (Chapter 10, "Gleaning from History") I went to the Bible for the teaching methods of Jesus and searched vintage books for the methodology of the Greeks, the Romans, the Hebrews, Martin Luther and others. The last educator examined in that book was Comenius (1592-1671). Here we begin with Milton (1608-1674). Once again my primary sources are antiquarian volumes. Most of the educators that I have researched agree on the following:

- Children are a gift from God.
- Parents are commanded to train their children for God.
- All education is for the individual, not for the state.
- All should have the opportunity to be educated.

John Milton
1608-1674

Best known for his *Paradise Lost,* Milton was already an accomplished scholar at the age of fifteen. Later he wrote a tract on educational reform. Its opening statement implies that the educator serves for ". . . the love of God and of mankind." The teacher molds human nature by "knowledge of God, love to God and hence imitation of God, until we become like God."[1]

Milton felt that being taught to appear to know was a root of all falsehood in life, society and professions. Today we have the deception of "teaching to the test" by teachers and cramming for tests by students, wherein knowledge departs when the test is completed.

Education should produce well-informed, moral citizens. The parents' good example readily motivates the young child with a desire for doing right, as children want to be just like their parents.

Ideas from Milton

- Point out and name objects as Baby is taught to speak: the knowledge of words is best obtained by the early knowledge of things.

- Begin educating with interesting books that invite study, provoke thought and encourage virtue. Language (literature) records the experience and traditions of other people and times and is how we acquire all information.

- Along with delightful books, provide careful instruction and explanation in order to stimulate love for learning and willful obedience. Teaching should arouse thought and exercise memory. If what is studied fails to become the property of the mind, learning is in vain.

- Review scriptures, times tables and other facts.

- Go over the same subject matter in greater depth. (See *Easy Homeschooling Techniques* and *The Well-Trained Mind*.)

- Study math daily.

- Study Scripture every evening. A habitual devotional time is crucial. Giving God unhurried time will honor Him as the Highest and instill honor for Him in your children.

- Begin with easy topics, but learn thoroughly.

- Do not force ". . . the empty wits of children to compose themes and essays . . ." on subjects of which they know nothing.[2]

- Teach your children to despise bad character.

- Most of all, incite to virtue and to a desire to make a mark in their lifetime and beyond.

John Locke
1632-1704

John Locke placed the formation of character much higher than simple learning, believing that the greatest aim of moral education is the conquest of self. "The great principle and foundation of all virtue lies in this, that a man is able to deny himself his own desires, cross his own inclinations and purely follow what reason directs as best, though the appetite lean the other way."[3]

To be successful, begin early. The first principle that must be implanted is that of submission to authority. The parent is in God's place on the earth. Training needs to be rigorous and yet not severe. Locke did not believe in corporal punishment, unless for sure obstinacy. Some behavior should be firmly stopped and consistently watched. This behavior ranges from the earliest signs of violence to a domineering attitude over siblings, playmates or even animals. Governing principles must be trained in the seemingly small matters of childhood. In Locke's understanding, morality would be more easily taught if the child were to suffer the natural consequences of his actions.

> Believe and speak the best of your child.

Do not warn the child of possible faults, as this indicates distrust. Stimulate that which is good in the child to prevent the entrance of evil. Locke said that when faced with an infraction we should express disbelief that the child is capable of wrong. When we are believing the best about the child, this is not deception.

When childhood gives way to youth, ☆ **the child is brought to right by treating him with respect** through necessary explanations. However, the early establishment of authority is the easiest way to obtain obedience, respect and love. Being harsh in rebuke forfeits respect, affection and benefit, and places the parent in a position inferior to the child.

Suggestions from Locke

- Get the attention of the scholar and create a love of learning by being consistently kind. The child will then want to please, as love begets love.

- Keep natural curiosity active by cooperative research and interaction.

- Do not introduce tedious subjects too soon; nevertheless, the child needs to discover that there is pleasure in intellectual exercise. (Locke believed that dry material just needed to be gotten through, giving the example of the study necessary as a doctor or lawyer.)

- Not all students need Latin. Begin French early so proper accents can be learned.

- Begin language study with conversation and translation, not with grammar.

- English grammar rules are not as important as correct speech.

- After oral composition, one should teach succinct and methodical written composition.

John Locke wrote *Some Thoughts Concerning Education* in 1693. The following excerpts are from that work.[4]

Learning must be had, but in the second place, as subservient only to greater qualities . . . gently correct and weed out any bad inclinations, and settle in him good habits. This is the main point, and this being provided for, learning may be had into the bargain.

Habits

What you think necessary for them to do, settle in them by an indispensable practice as often as the occasion returns; and, if it be possible, make occasions. This will beget habits in them, which, being once established, operate of themselves easily and naturally, without the assistance of the memory. But here let me give two cautions:

> Frame his manners, secure his innocence, cherish and nurse up the good.
>
> *Locke*

1) *The one is, that you keep them to the practice of what you would have grow into a habit in them by kind words and gentle admonitions, rather as [re]minding them of what they forget, than by harsh rebukes and chiding, as if they were willfully guilty.*

2) *Another thing you are to take care of is, not to endeavour to settle too many habits at once, lest by variety you confound them, and so perfect none.*

Manners

He that knows how to make those he converses with easy, without debasing himself to low and servile flattery, has found the true art of living in the world, and being both welcome and valued every where. Civility therefore is what in the first place should with great care be made habitual to children and young people.

The thing they should endeavor and aim at in conversation, should be to show respect, esteem and good-will, by paying to every one that common ceremony and regard which is in civility due to them. To do this, without a suspicion of flattery, dissimulation or meanness, is a great skill which good sense, reason and good company can only teach; but is of so much use in civil life, that it is well worth the studying.

> If children learn to love and respect others, it will be evident in their manners.

If I were to speak my mind freely, so children do nothing out of obstinacy, pride and ill-nature, it is no great matter how they put off their hats or make legs. If you can teach them to love and respect other people, they will, as their age requires it, find ways to express it acceptably to every one . . . . But where there is pride or ill-nature appearing in his carriage, there he must be persuaded or shamed out of it.

Though children, when little, should not be much perplexed with rules and ceremonious parts of breeding, yet there is a sort of unmannerliness very apt to grow up with young people, if not early restrained; and that is a forwardness to interrupt others that are speaking, and to stop them with some contradiction. . . .

I do not say this, that I think there should be no difference of opinions in conversation, nor opposition in men's discourses. . . . Tis not the owning one's dissent from another, that I speak against, but the manner of doing it. Young men should be taught not to be forward to interpose their opinions; unless asked, or when others have done, and are silent; and then only by way of enquiry, not instruction.

✔ Use portions of the above for copywork for the older child.

History

With geography, chronology in history ought to go hand in hand . . . Without these two, history, which is the great mistress of prudence and civil knowledge, and ought to be the proper study of a gentleman or man of business in the world; without geography and chronology, I say, history will be very ill retained and very little useful, but be only a jumble of matters of fact, confusedly heaped together without order or instruction. It is by these two, that the actions of mankind are ranked into their proper places of times and countries; under which circumstances, they are not only much easier kept in the memory, but in that natural order, are only capable to afford those observations which make a man the better and the abler for reading them.

Jean Jacques Rousseau
1712-1778

Rousseau's theories influenced a long line of educators, beginning with Pestalozzi, and continuing until this day. Rousseau received very limited moral training when young. He was so young when his mother died, he did not even remember her (*World Book,* 1930). As a youth, he was plagued with a number of "loose and vicious" habits. He took up with a promiscuous, illiterate woman. Their five children were completely abandoned and put in foundling homes.

Rousseau wrote a number of works, many of which were so radical they were banned or burned. Napoleon considered Rousseau's *Social Contract* the cause of the French Revolution (*World Book*) and this work became its textbook. Rousseau's theories bore bloody fruit and changed the politics of France and the entire Western world. His educational treatise and romance, *Emile* (1762), was also controversial. His arrest was ordered, but he left the country. In the introduction, Rousseau wrote:

> *Everything is good as it comes from the hands of the Author of Nature; but everything degenerates in the hands of man . . . . He overturns everything, disfigures every-thing; he loves deformity, monsters; he will have nothing as Nature made it, not even man; like a saddle-horse, man must be trained for man's service—he must be made over according to his fancy, like a tree in his garden.*[5]

Rousseau goes on to describe Emile's education:
1) Emile must be removed to the country where the corrupting influences of civilization are least concentrated.
2) His growth must be as nearly spontaneous as possible.
3) He must not learn to read until he is twelve years of age and then, read only a little.
4) His teacher must not exercise authority over him.
5) The teacher must not teach didactically, but only guide Emile

into contact with the world and nature. The child is to make the discoveries for himself.

6) The boy thinks that he is learning independently; however, the teacher is subtly controlling all of Emile's activities.

As a child, Emile is not hindered with duty, obligation, character, religion or manners. He is a totally free agent, not commanded to do anything, nor punished, nor taught. He learns personal responsibility, Rousseau wrote, by natural consequences. His is the outdoor life. He learns to draw by drawing from what he sees around him. Then at age

> The teacher subtly controls all of Emile's activities.

twelve, he learns to read. His chief novel is *Robinson Crusoe,* "that he may learn the delight and glory of irresponsible, natural life and the dignity and pleasure of self-help."[6]

Then, automatically, or so it seems, at the age of fifteen, the child becomes aware of his relationships to others and develops his moral and religious sentiments. How? He is brought into contact with humble and unfortunate people and all his selfishness dissipates—he becomes a youth with perfect moral character. Sure.

At this point I am thinking *Emile* is more fiction than philosophy. Emile is not instructed in the religion of any sect and particularly none that may be judgmental. He is then ready for his life mate. Enter Sophie, educated to be a woman, just as Emile was educated to be a man. Rousseau's ideas on female education do not reveal high estimates of womanhood. Emile is written in a clear, brilliant style, which may be the reason for its enduring influence. Its brightest feature is the love of nature pervading the book.

Vicesimus Knox
1752-1821

At twenty-nine, Vicesimus Knox published *Liberal Education* (1781), a protest against the innovations of his day. Rather than physical, philosophical and mathematical studies, Knox advocated classical learning because it:

- Opened doors to research and culture.
- Made a true gentleman, opening pleasures unknown to others.
- Produced enlargement, refinement and embellishment of the mind.

Knox compared the classically educated man to a polished precious stone, while others were only painted and garnished. This resulted from a disciplined study of philosophy, poetry and history, yet Knox saw this course as impractical before age nineteen, as all previous time was taken up learning the classical languages.

Languages

Throughout *Liberal Education,* Knox gives credit to the actual study of languages as producing the desired result. In other words, the mental discipline of learning the languages produces results greater than the knowledge of the languages themselves. Latin, and Latin grammar particularly, should be studied first. Knox thought that after just six months, the learner should go on to parsing (analyzing parts of speech) and construing (interpreting). He believed that all rules, in both Latin and English, should be learned. After Latin, he recommended Greek and French.

Classical Study Tips by Knox

- English should be acquired by reading the works of good authors: first Aesop, then history, then Plutarch.

- Themes should be written on the material covered.

- Geography should be studied with maps, not books. He thought map-drawing a waste of time.

- History should be read as recreation and not a subject.

- Euclid, astronomy and physics are best left for the university.

• Drawing should be taught only to those with an aptitude for it. (I believe ✿ **drawing** skills can be trained.)

Knox believed in early and rigorous memory training.

Beautiful passages should be studiously committed to memory or they will leave no more trace than the shadow of the summer cloud does on the landscape. Such passages should first be construed [analyzed], then learnt by heart. Habit will render it easy.[7]

He said subjects should be few, and for young children, "it is essential that tasks should be short—a little and with ease. The value is not the gain from one lesson, but in the habit, the constant growth and accumulation of power."[8]

Knox promoted eight grade levels, two exams per year and competition during daily lessons to spur to emulation. He had a high vision for education and believed that classical education was the best preparation for any employment above the low and mechanical. However, the route to his destination was not clear, nor did it seem readily available for all. He even admitted that his ideas were successful with only a few students.

Richard Lowell Edgeworth & Maria Edgeworth
1744-1817, 1767-1849

Richard Lowell Edgeworth and his daughter, Maria Edgeworth, published *Practical Education* in 1798, based on their own family's experiences. The Edgeworths thought one should take advantage of early childhood when the child is most curious and when he begins to question the workings of the world around him. To avoid disagreeable associations with learning, the Edgeworths promoted the play of kindergarten. Along with cutting and pasting, they wrote that the youngest student could begin picture study. The Edgeworths suggest copying art prints, even if the child's work is merely "random marks all over a sheet of paper."[9] I believe that even young children can do better than that and provide clear instructions in my book, *Easy Homeschooling Techniques.* For more extensive instruction see *Drawing With Children* by Mona Brooks.

The Edgeworths were unwilling to burden the young child with too many subjects. Keeping to one thing inspires the student with confidence in attainment and interest. "The pupil must be presented with little at a time, but it should be completely attained. . . . [The child's] attention must not be fatigued with variety."[10] Lessons should cover short periods, but the learner should be encouraged to put forth his utmost strength during that period.

> Knowledge cannot be attained without labor.
>
> *The Edgeworths*

The pupil must understand that knowledge cannot be obtained without labour. . . . A serious and strong effort for half an hour will do more in forming the habit of attention than the practice of assigning work that will last for hours.[11]

Progress is not nearly as important as maintaining the joy of learning and the desire to return to a lesson. Complete understanding is more important that speed or amount of work covered.

Phonics

"Do not be in a hurry . . . . When the vowel sounds are acquired, take the consonants, but do not give their names till the child has acquired their power." The Edgeworth's plan came to be called the "Phonic Method." Edgeworth objected to spelling books but thought that the words first taught should be those that appear frequently in the child's reading and conversation. Mistakes in writing can be pointed out and corrected. ". . . spelling is learned by the eye, hence the more they read and write, the greater their progress will be in spelling correctly."[12]

Books

The continuity of the ideas in books is more important than stopping every other word to look up meaning. "It is not verbal memory, but intelligence that should be cultivated."[13] "Great care should be taken in the selection of books, whether for reading or technical study. . . ."[14] Early reading books should never contain vice, wrongdoing or faults. Such books often put evil into the minds of children when it otherwise would not have entered. Selections should be free from deceit and from urging right actions by questionable motives. They should always be written in good English. The Edgeworths strongly condemned vulgar language and colloquialism in books.

Tips from the Edgeworths

• History must be presented without bias. The child can make his own rational judgments when given the true facts.

• Poetry should not be taught too early. Descriptive poetry demands little effort of attention and fails in training the intellect. It should be read only occasionally. More difficult poetry must always be accompanied by questioning and explanation to be profitable. When clearly understood, it may be committed to memory.

• Grammar should not be begun too early. Instruction should begin at the basics (subject, predicate; noun, verb) and go on to more complicated sentences as the child advances.

Regarding moral training, the Edgeworths believed that punishment should follow wrongdoing as a natural consequence. When commands are necessary, be sure you are willing to enforce them, for if you do not, you are training in disobedience. Reasoning with a young child is futile. Since they are not able to understand, explicit obedience must be required. Whenever we can use reason with an older child, we should never use force.

Johann Heinrich Pestalozzi
1746-1827

Pestalozzi's father was a physician of great intelligence, but died before Johann was six years of age. His grandfather was a country pastor and had a godly influence on the boy, as did his mother. "The pious example of his mother and the tranquil life he led with her, made the boy reflective and imaginative, while his soul became filled with great thoughts for the well-being of mankind."[15]

Motivated by this burning desire to relieve the burdened, Pestalozzi tried farming, ministry and law, before finding his calling as an educator. He gave up ministry because he felt inadequate in preaching, and law because he realized that human law could never do away with injustice. His farming venture was also philanthropic— he wanted to teach peasants better methods. Pestalozzi believed education would free the oppressed. His first educational endeavor was a forerunner of our technical schools.

Pestalozzi's philosophy of education stemmed from his own experiences. Pestalozzi said, "The only sure foundation upon which we may hope to secure national culture and elevate the poor is that of the home where the love of the father and mother is the ruling principle." As a child he "could not write, nor read, nor work accounts well" and was dismissed from a teaching position because of these deficiencies.

Pestalozzi was influenced by Rousseau and wanted to establish a "psychological method of instruction" that was in line with the laws of human nature. He placed a special emphasis on spontaneity and self-activity. He believed children should learn through the senses from real life, not through words or rote learning, and that they should be free to pursue their own interests and draw their own conclusions. They should not be given ready-made answers but should arrive at answers themselves. The child's powers of seeing, judging and reasoning should be cultivated and self-activity encouraged.

Although Pestalozzi disdained exact method, in his book, *How Gertrude Teaches her Children,* he attempts to explain his system as well as how to apply the ideas of Comenius and Rousseau. (His second literary work, *Leonard and Gertrude,* received a gold medal. It gives a picture of how a peasant woman blesses her family and her neighbors.)

The Home and Colonial School Society was the first school in England devoted to advancing the methods of Pestalozzi. In 1860, Charlotte Mason began her three-year training course there.[16] Pestalozzi's influence on Charlotte Mason can be seen in the first few principles of the following adaptation of a longer compilation of Pestalozzi's ideas by William H. Kilpatrick.[17]

- Personality is sacred.
- In each child is the promise of his potentiality.
- Love of those we would educate is essential.

Vintage books on the history of education tell us that Pestalozzi also believed:

- Children should be taught with other children.
- All knowledge is obtained through the senses by the self-activity of the child.
- Objects should be used freely, especially with young children.
- The mother is the natural educator of the child in the early years and she should be educated herself. "Maternal love is the first agent in education . . . through it the child is led to love and trust his Creator and his Redeemer."
- He used the phonics method, math manipulatives, relative grading (according to capacity of child) and taught all subjects through doing.

In my opinion, the great esteem placed upon Pestalozzi as educator is a mistake, and his doctrines—still prevalent today—have weakened our educational systems with their turn from literary learning. The most important idea we can harvest from Pestalozzi is that which animated his life's work—his loving commitment to people and their well-being.

Samuel Wilderspin
1792-1866

Do you think today's preschools for three- to five-year-old children are a new thing? Infant Schools actually began in the early 1800s and were similar to today's early preschools or daycare centers. However, Samuel Wilderspin's purpose was morality (based on his Swedenborgian beliefs[19]). Wilderspin thought that the schools were needed to give more supervision than the busy mother could provide at home. Children were taught what was useful and helpful but the primary aim was to form within the child good habits and a cheerful disposition. The child would thus be prevented from acquiring bad habits and would be trained in morality and character. Wilderspin's leading idea was to adapt the teaching to the nature of the child.

The children remained in the school for two or three years, after which they were admitted to a more advanced school, where they were taught to read, write and do arithmetic. The girls also learned to sew. The primary objectives, however, remained the same.

Robert Owen—founder of the Infants Schools in Britain—said:

> *The children are received into a preparatory or training school at the age of three, in which they are perpetually superintended, to prevent them acquiring bad habits, to give them good ones, and to form their dispositions to mutual kindness and a sincere desire to contribute all in their power to benefit each other. These effects are chiefly accomplished by example and practice, precept being found of little use, and not comprehended by them at this early age.*[20]

Although the original purpose of the infants schools was moral and physical training, many deteriorated into either places of amusement or—the complete opposite—schools where dry, hard, scientific words took the place of ideas and the physical world.

Charles Mayo
1792-1846

In 1836, the Home and Colonial School Society was formed in for the purpose of promoting Pestalozzi's pedagogy and also for "fixing" the infant school system. This was where Charlotte Mason's received her training.

> Head, Hands, Heart—
> Learning, Work, Character

Charles Mayo, with his sister Elisabeth, interpreted Pestalozzi's theories for England. Pestalozzi's premises were, in a nutshell, that the child should observe with accuracy and then express his observation with correctness. Charles Mayo expanded this idea, stating that education should be religious, moral, organic, active, harmonious and progressive. The Society emphasized Scripture and evangelism.

The primary aim of education is religious. The goal for this life is that the student be conformed to the image of God. Because God's love is what transforms, the teacher is to do all that is needed to model this love to the student. Our standard is the Gospel, our example, the Savior. Morality is to pervade the home and school. Exceptions are not allowed. Morality, character and knowledge are amassed through the process of building from within. We cultivate dispositions, form principles and establish habits.

Education is ". . . powerless to change the heart or improve the life if it is not accompanied by the direct influence of the Holy Spirit."[18] Likewise, our own efforts will be powerless without God's sure guidance. Education is not just memory work, using the Word or knowing doctrines, but the supernatural transformation of a life, initiated by the transforming character of the Word of God.

The Home and Colonial Society believed that the most important first premises to teach are 1) God's character, 2) His abhorrence of sin, 3) His mercy through Christ, 4) the child's duties and his relationship to God—which together would bring the child to a saving knowledge of Jesus Christ.

To overcome selfishness, the child should be induced to share or yield the best part, or that which he desires. Yet there must also be liberty. The child must learn to make the appropriate choices for himself. This will-exercise forms godly habits and character that will be his compass when he leaves the more restrictive influence of the home. How does he learn this? Be alert for consequences and blessings and point them out to your child. When good deeds are praised, that is a good harvest. There are other good and bad harvests that come as a result of any act.

Head, Hands, Heart—Learning, Work, Character—all areas are to be developed and are to work together for the glory of God. Education should be progressive, always leading to a higher level of knowledge, obedience, character and service.

Tips from The Society

1) *Teach your youngest child about his dear Heavenly Father.*
   - Lead him to talk about God.
   - Observe His works together.
   - Emphasize God's power in creation.
   - Point out God's goodness in the workings of the earth and the weather.
   - Speak of God's love as shown by the love of family and friends.
   - Let him see the love of God in your love for him.
   - Carefully impress these things by repetition.

2) *Next use Scripture stories and Bible prints.*
   - Check your library for art books covering Bible subjects.
   - Observe these art prints to awaken curiosity and to engage attention.
   - Encourage your child to tell about what he sees.
   - Write down these oral compositions.

3) *Teach deeper Scripture.*
- Use Bible storybooks and the Bible itself.
- Study histories, character passages, moral duties and natural history.
- Allow your child to narrate as you transcribe.

Johann Friedrich Herbart
1776-1841

Herbart's mother was a great influence on his education. She even studied Greek with him. She was gentle and yet firm in discipline. Eventually Herbart's parents separated. After University and a short time as a tutor, he went for further study. Herbart knew Pestalozzi and was impressed with him. It is said that Herbart elevated education to a science. It seems to me that he was instrumental in complicating a simple process. Yet, he had a worthy goal: "Well-rounded men, fit for all the duties of life; men well-developed physically, intellectually, morally and spiritually."[21]

Friedrich Froebel
1782-1852

Friedrich Froebel is considered the father of the kindergarten. Like Pestalozzi, whose work influenced him greatly, Froebel's education was neglected in his early years. Although he began his four years of school at age ten, it does not appear that he made much progress. Like Pestalozzi, Froebel attempted various short-lived enterprises until finding his niche in education. Froebel said of Pestalozzi, "He set one's soul on fire for a higher and nobler life, though he had not made clear or sure the exact road toward it, nor indicated the means whereby to attain it."[22]

Froebel's philosophy is found in *Education of Man.* He said that a purpose of the kindergarten was to lead children "to the origin of all life and to union with Him."[23] However, in 1851 the Prussian government prohibited kindergartens as "socialistic . . . the aim of which is to teach children atheism."[24] Even into the 1900s, Prussia did not recognize the kindergarten as an educational institution. Froebel, nevertheless, did recognize the mother as the natural teacher and he thought it her duty to fit herself for the sacred responsibility that God placed on her.

Horace Mann
1796-1859

Horace Mann believed that a free, intelligent and moral people could only be realized by public education. Mann nearly single-handedly enabled nation-wide public education. He did a colossal work in drawing together funding and administration. Although he prophetically said there should be ". . . a free, straight, solid pathway by which [the child] can walk directly up from the ignorance of an infant to a knowledge of the primary duties of man,"[25] he could not have imagined the scope of today's public education from kindergarten through high school. He established free schools, founded normal schools to train teachers, encouraged milder forms of discipline, and improved schoolhouses.

John Dewey
1859-1952

John Dewey's theories shaped education throughout the twentieth-century, seriously weakening it. Look around to see the fruit of his methods. Except for a remnant, Dewey's highly accepted theories destroyed the "thinking man." John Dewey disdained traditional education and was ". . . especially critical of the rote learning of facts in schools and argued that children should learn by experience."[26]

> *The child is the starting point, the centre, and the end. His development, his growth, is the ideal. . . . To the growth of the child all studies are subservient; they are instruments valued as they serve the needs of growth. Personality,*

character, is more than subject matter. Not knowledge or information, but self-realisation, is the goal. To possess all the world of knowledge and lose one's own self is as awful a fate in education as in religion.[27]

"He wanted a classroom where children could move about, form groups, plan and execute activities, in short, learn for themselves under the direction and guidance of the teacher."[28]

Dewey's Educational Philosophy

- Students are to be trained to be productive members of the group.
- Students are to be stimulated to act for the good of the group.
- Educational activity—even what the child learns and how much he accomplishes— must arise from the child's desires, not from external structure or preset subject matter.
- Education is to be project-oriented.
- The child's individual tendencies are to be directed toward co-operative living.

> Dewey was a Socialist and member of the ACLU.

Dewey was a member of the American Civil Liberties Union, the Socialist Party and the Progressive Party; he also supported Robert La Follette in his attempts to become president.[29] La Follette was anti-war in his sentiments and married to a feminist. His presidential campaign (1924) was supported by unions and the Socialist Party. La Follette thought highly of atheist Robert G. Ingersoll.[30]

We Close the Volumes

The late afternoon sun is warm as we turn the last page of the last volume. We have looked at some educators worthy of emulation, and others whose ideology we may wish to avoid. We have much to contemplate, and perhaps you have gleaned ideas that you can use in your own school.

•• Do your own study of the history of education. See ☞ **Endnotes** or go to *www.google.com* to search for information on the educator of your choice.

6

Raising the Standard
Through Recitation and Study Techniques

*W*e arrive at the bright white schoolhouse and enter its hushed interior. The schoolmaster welcomes us. After inviting us to sit near the front of the classroom, he begins our lessons by writing the following list on the blackboard in his attractive Spencerian hand.

The Evidences of Education

- Power and habit of reflection.
- Efficiency or the power to do (productivity).
- Correctness and precision in the use of the mother tongue.
- Refined and gentle manners, resulting from fixed habits of thought and action.
- Sound standards of appreciation of beauty and of worth and a character based on those standards.

Continuing our learning session, the schoolmaster articulates:
Today we will examine an educational process through which many of these purposes will be achieved. We will look at recitation—its definition, its purposes, its characteristics, its standards and its practice in the schools.

Recitation Defined

Recitation is "the rehearsal of a prepared lesson by students before their instructor."[1] The material used might be an excerpt from a book, learned facts or knowledge from a previous lesson, something memorized or an original work. The recitation may even be answers to the teacher's questions but more likely a talk based on a number of pre-assigned questions.

For proper recitation, there is preparatory study, well-thought-out editing and polished expressive delivery. In these things, recitation goes beyond the highly effective, yet informal, practice of narration. It contrasts substantially with rote learning in which the student merely memorizes key points that he soon forgets.

Purposes

The recitation is the greatest medium for instruction, especially for the young student who is not yet able to write fluently. It is a perfect tool for early education. Through recitation, the student acquires power, skill and permanent knowledge. Recitation places the entire responsibility on the child to know the facts, thus it is a form of testing, demonstrating what the child knows and indicating how well he has learned the current subject matter.

> Recitation sets the tone for excellence at the portal of learning.

Recitation prepares for written work in all subjects. Mathematical skill, for instance, is the result of mental exercises. Oral drill will give the capacity to calculate accurately and rapidly.

Although recitation does result in knowledge of the subject matter, ☆ **the most notable and enduring result is a distinct quality of the mind.** This mind will receive knowledge readily and be quick to discern truth from error. Tyron Edwards, 19th century theologian—and Jonathan Edward's great-grandson—said, "The great end of education is to discipline rather than to furnish the mind; rather than fill it with the accumulations of others." Our purpose is not to fill the pupil's mind with facts but to encourage love of the subject and of the thought process which opens the door to knowledge, wisdom and character.

Recitation enables the pupil's life-long habits of thought and expression. Will his thoughts be accurate? Will his expression be clear and vigorous? Recitation also inspires the child with a love for learning. Do we not love doing the things we do well? Contributing to this is the immediate feedback of recitation.

Goals

It is advantageous for the instructor to set goals for recitation. The aims of recitation might be to:
- Cultivate the power of expression.
- Aid in comprehension and memory retention.
- Stimulate study, research, thought and motivation.
- Help the child become comfortable before others.
- Form habits of attention, control and concentrated effort.
- Assess knowledge, skill, power, preparation and viewpoint.
- Identify weak areas, such as pronunciation.

Standards

The first requirement of formal recitation is formal discipline because the recitation is judged by quietness and order; the children not reciting are to be absolutely still. A consistent schedule again comes to our aid; with an established time for study and recitation, the child—and the child's mind—will be trained to the necessary silence. ☆ **Right action repeated forms good habits; habit forms character.**

The distinguishing mark of recitation is proper English, with an emphasis on clarity. Correct posture is also important, with the standing position as most common and most desirable.

It is an advantage for the recitation to be challenging because children do only what they are required to do. Minimal requirements yield minimal results. The best recitation ". . . arouses, stirs, stimulates. It fills the mind and heart with a burning zeal. It lights the torches of desire with a never-quenching flame of enthusiasm."[2]

Characteristics

- *Clarity.* The recitation should be clear, strong, logical, systematic, complete and to the point—much like good writing.

- *Brisk mental movement.* The recitation should be well-thought-out and carried rapidly from point to point, showing brisk mental movement. (More below under "Technique.")

- *Brevity.* The recitation should be brief. This is especially important with younger children. Build confidence and excellence with small successes. The short recitation is generally better than a long one. If the piece is an original essay, the piece should be well-edited so only the best, clearest and most forceful phrasing remains.

- *Adapted to the child's ability.* The material needs to be "just right" for the child. Yet, it is better to err on the side of too difficult because:

The racehorse that is never pushed to his best efforts seldom increases his speed. So the little child that works at a pace of effort too easy for him gets little return. Much of the ordinary schoolwork is so easy for the child that the effort is almost without recompense. We classify and simplify, we analyze and dilute the child's mental food, until there is nothing left for his mental digestive apparatus to do. We waste much valuable time trying to teach him what he already knows, to show him what he sees and in trying to explain what he clearly understands.[3]

The Teacher's Part

The teacher who expects and accepts imperfect prepara-
tion, superficial work, a hazy conception of truth and a
careless expression of it, will generally get them . . . but
blessed is the child who comes under the influence of a
teacher who demands vigorous work, thorough prepara-
tion and clearness of comprehension.[4]

The teacher sets the tone for the school. Be patient and loving;
expect excellence, insist upon it, never teach without it. You set the
example for study. In the early years, study along with your children,
teaching them where to seek out facts and what resources to use.
Give them ample opportunities to report and recite on the topics
they are interested in. They will develop lifetime learning skills.

The mechanical teacher pours in the facts. The experimental
teacher tries everything with no definite plan or aim. The philosophical teacher looks on her work from a higher standpoint,
considering the end desired, using materials and methods to reach
that end.

Essentials

The two essentials of recitation are *interest* and *attention.* Attention
is the effort of the mind to know more. You will not gain the attention of your pupils by commanding, punishing, pleading, rewarding
or repeating yourself. Repetition actually draws attention away from
the subject at hand. Attention is severed in a split-second when the
child recognizes that he is hearing what he has already heard.
Surprise and change will keep the child attentive, but the most
enduring and natural way to gain attention is to create interest.

An enthusiastic teacher will inspire enthusiasm in her students.
The teacher, first of all, should exhibit interest in the topic or at least
cultivate interest in the process of seeing her pupils learn. Interest is
the root from which attention springs.

Gaining Interest

- Interest can be stimulated by using a current event. Study the Constitution and government at the time of an election and inauguration, earthquakes after a recent tremor or the culture or country where an event is taking place. In this case, the teaching of the "old" arises from the "new."

- The teaching of the "new" arising from the "old" can also stimulate interest. This is when something new is introduced into a study of the familiar. This might be a new concept in math or additional interesting details about a topic or person already studied.

- Interest is also ignited as an older child embraces a goal (such as college, career, ministry or even high school graduation) and tackles a subject—whether agreeable or not—as a stepping stone to that goal.

Technique

Brisk mental movement characterizes the recitation. Change tends to arouse the mind, keep curiosity active and attract attention. You can train this strong and rapid thought process by a series of quick questions, suggestions, new insights, explanations and directions—all the while being sensitive to the thought rate of your student, gradually increasing his mental speed so that he will learn to think and recite in this manner. Such a recitation develops alertness of mind, quick perception and a prompt mental response. "The recitation should be the birthplace of living thought, not a morgue filled with dead thought."[5]

> Recitation is "brain training."

✔ For an impromptu recitation, ask the student to rise, then direct a question or a series of questions at him. Require complete sentences. Alternately, you may ask the question first and then call on a student. Use the thought-provoking questions, "Why?" and "How?" more than "What?" "When?" and "Where?" Your questions should require thought and creativity. For example, do not ask, "What happened during the first battle of the Civil War?" but ask, "What do you think might have happened had the Civil War not been fought? Discuss the social and religious aspects."
  - Ask questions.
  - Make suggestions.
  - Maintain variety.
  - Keep sessions short.
  - Bring in an interesting anecdote.
  - Call upon pupils to recite without notice.
  - Illuminate the most appealing aspect of the topic.

A Recitation Idea

1) Assign a topic.
2) The student researches the topic.
3) The student tells all he knows about that topic.

Speech

Good speech is important in recitation and contributes to a rewarding and useful life. A person will speak many more words in his lifetime than he will write. Robert Louis Stevenson said, "The problem of education is twofold: first to know, and then to utter. Everyone who lives any semblance of an inner life thinks more nobly and profoundly than he speaks."

Speech, in recitation, can be divided into four equally important components. If one area is lacking, the entire presentation will be less than it can be.

Components of Speech

1) *Thoughtful Preparation.* The recitation must arise from clear and logical thought. The pupil should know the subject matter well and think each sentence before speaking. If necessary, he should pause to form the sentence in his mind. (Proper pauses are an effective speech technique.)

2) *Natural Yet Necessary Bodily Movement.* Recitation traditionally was marked with no action, only proper carriage and deportment. Modern speech giving is almost always accentuated by natural movement. Movement can be forward, backward and side to side. Gestures, including pointing, should be natural and—to avoid appearing awkward—should precede the part of the speech related to the motion.

3) *Proper Language Usage.* The language used should indicate mastery of the mother tongue. Address problems in your children's speech when they are young, and correct them. Do not overwhelm your child but focus on one area at a time until that area is mastered.

4) *Clear, Controlled and Varied Voice.* The voice should be clear and pleasant. It should not be too deep, too loud, too quiet, dull, nasal or monotone. A full controlled voice must emanate from a firm abdomen and diaphragm. The chin must be up. The student should exhibit variety in tone and speed of delivery, using proper pauses. ☆ **Teach by example, always speaking clearly, especially with young children.** (See "Proper English," below, for more on language usage and clarity.)

✔ Score speakers in the classroom, in church, etc. based on the four elements with "1" being the poorest and "25" being the best for each element. Add the scores together get the total score for each speaker.

Practice

For speech practice, use individual scriptures, poems or other passages of literature. If the selection is memorized, the child can focus on the other elements of speech as above. Speech should be taught every day, either directly or indirectly. Never allow sloppy speech. What you do now regarding speech will make a difference in your child's future.

Exercises

- Take a deep breath, tightening and then releasing the breath gradually while speaking a short sentence.
- Speak the consonants distinctly. For example, "b" does not say "bu."
- Practice short vowel sounds. When these sounds are mastered, begin pronouncing short words and then longer words individually and in unison.
- Next, drill sentences, emphasizing a different word each time.
- Choose a poem and have the students recite after the teacher, one line at a time.

Proper English

We study English to cultivate a taste for good literature and to achieve the highest possible capability in the art of expression. The learning of English not only begins with, but also ends in, reading, writing and speaking. The ability to use the mother tongue correctly and fluently with power and ease is a great accomplishment and the distinctive mark of recitation. Expression must rely on habit because in the rapid discourse of recitation, the mind is busy at thought.

Training Proper English

- The teacher should be the model of clear and correct speech from the earliest age. If the teacher is accurate, strong, easy and elegant in her use of language, so much the better.

- Expose your child to a rich and varied feast of fine literature. This exposure creates conditions where absorption of good English automatically takes place.

No other agency [but literature] is so potent in the enrich-ment and cultivation of the child's habitual use of English. . . . Literature is the treasure-house of the race. It contains the choicest gems of truth and beauty, phrased by the high priests of thought and expression. It has elements of culture which the formal study of language can never give. It touches the emotional nature of the child, cultivates the taste, appeals to the artistic sense, stirs his creative faculty and reacts upon his whole spiritual life.[6]

- Increased vocabulary results in high scores on college entrance tests, as well as being an aid to better expression. A large vocabulary increases spontaneously in proportion to the quan-tity of fine literature used. However, your child could keep a vocabulary notebook in which he writes the definitions of unknown words.

- Place an object or a painting before the child. Train the child to observe the size, shape, color and other characteristics. Have him describe it orally, emphasizing minute detail. Have him tell what the artist was trying to communicate and also what his own imagination suggests. When you touch the imagination, you release the powers of expression.

- Tell or read a fascinating story in faultless English. This will enrich both vocabulary and morals. Then let the pupil retell the story using as much choice language as necessary.

> Our children must be inspired to be the best they can be.

Regional or national accents add charm and personality. Instead of attempting to remove the accent, work on clarity (speaking each letter clearly). If others cannot understand you, it could be that you are speaking too rapidly.

It seems almost impossible to overcome the model of language that the child hears most often. Locale, extended family or even a parent can form a negative grammar imprint on the child's brain. In these cases, ✭ **the proper use of language must be stressed often enough and early enough—before the other influences have made their mark.** The child should be taught that proper expression is expected from the educated young man and young lady.

Overcoming Poor English

- Speak or write correctly, ten times, a phrase or word that has been used incorrectly.
- Begin a sentence with a noun, not a pronoun. Use "Dad" or "Mr. Smith" instead of "He."
- Avoid contractions. "I seen" is learned from hearing "I've seen" spoken indistinctly (as it usually is). Instead, use "I saw" or "I have seen."
- Use "The children were" not "The children was."

Training to Think

A composition is distinguished from a mere report of facts by originality of thought and expression. A daily composition springs from reflection and helps develop the thinking skills as the pupil examines, compares, discovers, concludes and states. If the composition is in the argumentative form, it is one of the greatest agencies in training the child to think, because this form of writing sets forth the writer's conclusions, opinions and arguments.

A preferred composition is on the day's reading. Choose good materials. Feed the child's precious mind whole foods. When your student is required to express an author's ideas in his own words, he must assimilate, dissect, reach conclusions and form opinions.

Study

Study and preparation are an integral part of the formal recitation. Times tables and Bible verses must be memorized. The report must be researched. The book must be read. Study is not something to be dreaded, for "the mind was made for truth . . . the greatest enjoyment and the chief employment of man are found in the exercise of the inherent power of the mind to seek, to discover and to understand."[7]

Study is an act of the mind and an act of the will—we must bring our thoughts into captivity to the subject at hand. Concentration is acquired by successes from similar efforts made in the past. Study should not focus on memorization or words but on ideas. Discipline, knowledge and character have been called the "triple crown of education" and should be the purpose of study.

1) *Discipline.* The well-formed mind sees clearly, thinks profoundly, reasons accurately and analyzes logically. Discipline is key. The most fruitful study is self-directed study. To train to be self-directed is to train for life-long education. Self-directed study is trained by a system of assignments and accountability. Encourage, enable and enforce independent study by your children. Assign or allow them choose a topic, then require research and reporting that is always reviewed and accessed.

2) *Knowledge.* Learning is like nutrition. The mind grows and must be fed. Acquired knowledge fills the mind. The more the mind is used and grows, the more knowledge it desires.

3) *Character.* Character is the most important aim of study. Character is shaped indirectly because study develops patience, perseverance, courage, self-reliance, reliance on God and self-respect. Study forms habits and reveals truths. As truths are contemplated, minds and hearts are drawn to the Author of truth. The Author of truth thus imparts character to the child.

4 Step Study Technique

1) *Learn the facts.* Read thoughtfully and carefully, attempting to discover the leading thought. Write it down if you need to. Do not memorize, but know.

2) *Reflect.* Seek to know what the main fact means and teaches. Think about the topic. Look for similarities or differences, subdivisions and other relationships. Now the portion studied is ready to be ❀ **outlined**, as the student unifies closely related truths into groups. They must scrutinize principles, statements, definitions and other elements until they are understood. Knowing the leading thought will help the memory, knowing what it means will build understanding and knowledge, while the entire process of learning changes character.

3) *Verify.* Double-check the facts. Examine maps and charts. Go to other books and source documents. Although this sounds difficult, it is the enjoyable pursuit of knowledge because it is inspired by curiosity. Verifying establishes the fact as truth, gives the mind a clearer view of the subject, fixes the fact more firmly, makes the mind stronger and more cautious, gives self-reliance, and makes truth and reason the standards of judgment.

4) *Repeat.* In the oral recitation or the written report, the student makes the knowledge permanent.

Some of the above steps can be done in a less formal learning situation, such as during family read-aloud sessions. We did steps one and two with our *Macbeth* study.

Study Requirements

1) Good health and comfort.
2) Fresh air of the right temperature.
3) Quiet.
4) Regular habits and hours for sleep, exercise and study.

21st Century Study

Recitation is not only a highly useful educational tool in the formal presentation, but enables permanent learning when used for study. The following excerpt from "Memory and Related Learning Principles,"[8] specifies why, based on brain research, the recitation is such an important learning technique and how to use it for study.

> There is no principle that is more important or more effective than recitation for transferring material from the short-term memory to the long-term memory. . . . Vocal— "out loud"—recitation is usually the most effective single technique for review because it employs more of the senses than any other review technique (utilizing both auditory and vocal senses).
>
> As you recite . . . you are holding each idea in mind for the four or five seconds that are needed for the temporary memory to be converted into a permanent one. In other words, the few minutes that it takes for you to review and think about what you are trying to learn is the minimum length of time that neuroscientists believe is necessary to allow thought to go into a lasting, more easily retrievable memory.

Procedure

Recitation is simply saying aloud the ideas that you want to remember. For example, after you have gathered your information in note form and have categorized and clustered your items, you recite them. Here's how: . . . cover your notes, then recite aloud the covered material. After reciting, expose the notes and check for accuracy. You should not attempt to recite the material word-for-word; rather your reciting should be in the words and manner that you would ordinarily use if you were explaining the material to a friend. When you can say it, then you know it.

Process

Recitation transfers material to the secondary or long-term memory. While you are reading the words in a sentence or paragraph, the primary memory (short-term memory) holds them in mind long enough for you to gain the sense of the sentence or paragraph. However, the primary memory has a very limited capacity, and as you continue to read, you displace the words and ideas of the initial paragraphs with the words of subsequent paragraphs. This is one reason for not remembering everything in the first part of the chapter by the time we reach the end of the chapter when we read continually without taking a break or taking time to review what we have already read. It is only when we recite or contemplate the idea conveyed by a sentence or paragraph that the idea has a chance (not guaranteed) of moving on into the secondary memory (a long-term storage facility). All verbal information goes first into the primary memory (short-term memory). When it is rehearsed (recited), part of it goes into

> Recitation moves the subject into the long-term memory.

our secondary (long-term) memory. The rest of it, usually the part we are least interested in, returns to the primary memory and is then forgotten. ★ **Whether new information is "stored" or "dumped" depends, then, on our reciting it out loud and on our interest in the information.**

After seven days, without review, students remembered 33% of the material. With review, the students remembered 83% of the material. After 63 days those who had not reviewed only remembered 14%, while those who had reviewed remembered a significant 70%. When we know something about a topic it is easier to learn and retain new information about it. This is why it is important to retain "old learnings."

Over-Study

Even though a person continues to study, he may expect to encounter periods when there seems to be little or no gain. Such plateaus in learning may be due to several causes such as fatigue, loss of interest or diminishing returns from using the same inefficient methods. Another explanation of plateaus is that they represent pauses between stages of understanding. When the student acquires a new insight, he can move on. Sometimes the lower stage of an understanding or a skill may actually interfere with progress to a higher level. [For instance, in learning to read, there is a changeover from a focus on letters to a focus on words.]

The important thing is to recognize that plateaus or periods of slow learning are inevitable, and they should not discourage the student unduly. Learning may still be taking place, but at a slower pace. Recognizing that he is at

> Both the rate of learning and the rate of retention can be improved with practice.

a plateau, the student should first try to analyze and improve his study methods, if possible. Sometimes, however, an incorrect mental set may be interfering with the necessary perception of new relationships. Sometimes slow learning may simply be due to fatigue. In either of these circumstances the most efficient procedure may be to drop the activity temporarily and return to it later, after a good night's rest.

The rate at which a student learns depends upon his learning ability, but slow learners remember just as well as fast learners, provided that they have learned the material equally well. The reason a bright student may do better on examinations is that he has learned the subject matter more effectively within the time available. But if a slower student spends enough time on his studies, he can retain every bit as much as the faster student. Fortunately, there is evidence that both rate of learning and rate of retention can be improved with practice.

Neuro-scientists have discovered ways to test electrical or chemical changes in the brain when students study or read difficult material for too long without stopping. They call this Neuro-Transmitter Depletion. B.F Skinner and other experts have concluded that the average student cannot study difficult matter or the same subject for more than four hours a day, even with short breaks every hour. Intelegen, Inc. suggests breaks of at least ten minutes every hour. After four consecutive hours, efficiency and memory suffer.

If one studies the same subject too long, fatigue, boredom, sometimes slight disorientation may occur. It is a common result of too much consecutive study when even the most simple concept begins not to make sense any longer. The monitoring of brain activity and chemical changes indicate that studying too long results in a depletion of chemicals in the brain cells necessary for efficient processing of information. . . .

Over-Learning

After you have recited a lesson long enough to say it perfectly, if you continue reciting it a few times more, you will over-learn it. A well known psychologist and researcher, Ebbinghaus, has reported that each additional recitation (after you really know the material) engraves the mental trace deeper and deeper, thus establishing a base for long-term retention. For many people, over-learning is difficult to practice because by the time they achieve bare mastery, there is little time left and they are eager to drop the subject and go on to something else.

☆ **But reciting the material even just one more time significantly increases retention, so try to remember this and utilize the technique when you can.**

Historical Recitation

By 1836 almost every white child on Long Island (NY) attended school.[9]

You went to learn enough math to help do the business ledger, enough reading to comprehend the Bible. . . . It was reading, writing, recitation. Spelling was a cornerstone subject, taught by rote. You said the word out loud and clapped your hand to each letter . . . .[10]

Public education moved westward with the pioneers across America. In the 1880s math problems had to be calculated in the head, without the aid of fingers or other objects for counting. The importance of arithmetic was emphasized by the fact that it was always studied early in the school day while the pupil's mind was fresh. Lessons were recited from youngest to oldest grades.

The pedagogy books of this period all emphasized a daily writing lesson. One author suggested that it was best taught at the end of the day as a rest from more active mental work. After the pupils had been at their seats awhile, their muscles and nerves would be quieted.

> *In 1904, a typical school day began at 8:30 a.m. with the ringing of the school bell. The curriculum focused on memorization and recitation. Textbooks and teachers stressed patriotism and moral values. Subjects might be reading, writing, arithmetic, geography, spelling, grammar, physiology, hygiene, history and sometimes music. Time was allotted in class for doing lessons so that there would be time to do chores at home.*[11]

Schoolmaster Strickler[12]

Jakob Strickler was schoolmaster at the school where the author of *Heidi* learned her ABCs. In 1808 he attended a four-week training course and in the fall of that year initiated a new teaching method in accordance with the principles detailed in Heinrich Pestalozzi's *Neue Pädagogik.*

Pastor Schweitzer, head of the school, praised Schoolmaster Strickler: "He is very loving of the children. He invests all of his diligence and loyalty in the them...."[13] Here is Schoolmaster Strickler's schedule:

- *9:00—9:30* Drill in mental arithmetic.

- *9:30—10:00* Alphabet training (phonics) was given to the first grade. Letters were drawn on the blackboard, beginning with the vowels followed by the consonants. Gradually the pupils were shown how syllables and short words were formed from the letters. (This method of ❀ **phonics teaching** is described in detail in *Easy Homeschooling Techniques.*) The student then copied his lesson from the board into individual notebooks. This accustomed the child to taking notes and keeping notebooks.

- *10:00—10:30* Blackboard instruction was given to the children in the next group (those who had mastered the ABCs). Schoolmaster Strickler emphasized simple, monosyllabic word formation with particular focus on root and stem words. This training continued as the students learned prefixes and suffixes and the resulting multi-syllabic words formed by them.

- *10:30* Time was spent with the next-level students—those who had achieved a level of reading capability. Schoolmaster Strickler would read an article or other text aloud to them in a clear fashion. Then he would familiarize his pupils with the key words and adjectives in the article and discuss its content.

- *12:00 noon* Homework assignments were given out and explained to those who could not yet write. Those who had achieved a level of writing ability worked on their compositions. Then they might do a reading exercise, study or memorize a selection for recitation period.

- *2:00—3:00* Recitation. Each class, one after the other, listened to the lessons of the other classes. The children of each class recited and articulated to the others. Their materials were the New Testament, *Kinderfreund* by Professor Schulthessen and Steinmüller's *Schulbuch*.

Examinations

Examinations were also oral. First, the younger students were presented for examination followed by those who had already learned much of reading, writing, arithmetic and singing. Then came the presentations by the pupils who had learned their assigned songs by heart. Also undertaken were reading exercises from the New Testament, a review of report cards and more readings, this time from Waser's pamphlets and from Schulthessen's *Kinderfreund.* Then a grammatical review of the material read. Lastly there was a recitation in writing principles and calculating.

It was noted that several six- to eight-year-old pupils had acquired attractive handwriting and did particularly well in reciting beautiful music. Some attributed their accomplishments to the reward system established by the regional school authority; the students were given one to five shillings in accordance to their exam performance.

Rote learning continued for several years. By the end of the 1810—1811 school year, the class had memorized 1,416 text extracts, 1,216 songs and 200 pages from *Gessner's Lesson Book*. It was noted that one had be patient with the behavior of the boys until they advanced to a more elevated and courteous level of conduct. Many of the boys and girls, however, distinguished themselves with good behavior and exemplary comportment.

An Efficient Technique

During the time when recitation was widely in use, some questioned whether classroom recitation suppressed the child's thoughts and feelings. Were the pupil's thoughts actually elsewhere? Were the recitations merely rote displays? Was the knowledge stated soon forgotten? Were the children responsible and active in learning? Some spoke of the recitation as merely an oral examination, while others said that recitation wasted time because many were silent while only one was tested (overlooking the fact that each child was learning from the example of the one reciting and from the content of the recitation). These concerns brought the educational establishment to abandon recitation for new methods, giving the results we see today. In the past, pupils were well-taught in eight years or less; today we keep our children in schools for far too many years, continually repeating easy subject matter. Some children are left behind because they have not been taught well. This is not efficient for governments, nor beneficial for

> Recitation was abandoned for new methods, giving the results we see today.

children. We should expect more. We can raise standards and promote excellence in education by establishing a daily recitation routine in our schools.

7

Reaping from Reviews

Most books hide kernels of gold amidst much chaff. In my reviewing, I first select the most promising books, then winnow the chaff so that only the gold remains. What is left is the essence of the book—the helpful ideas. If there is a lot of gold, such as in *A Charlotte Mason Companion,* I select a portion for my review. Unless otherwise noted, quotations are from the book reviewed.

Hints on Child Training
H. Clay Trumball

H. Clay Trumball lived over one hundred years ago. In *Hints on Child Training* he gives grandfatherly advice to another generation, reinforcing the practices we know in our heart to be right.

What is training? Training is the shaping, developing and controlling of feelings, thoughts, words and ways. "The essence of training is causing another to do. . . . Training gives skill. Training shapes the habits. Training and teaching must go on together in the wise upbringing of any and every child." It is the parents' duty, privilege and challenge to train their children. Training is the most important task of our lives. Teaching—the world's priority—is secondary.

*They [The children] must learn how to do things which they
do not want to do, when those things ought to be done: to
get up in the morning at a proper hour, to go to bed at a
fitting time, to eat at proper times—and proper foods.
There must be a place for tasks and for times of study
under the pressure of stern duty—it is not enough to have
children learn only the lessons which they enjoy.*

Training can be done most effectively and easily with a young child;
however even a young adult can be trained. As an example, consider
the maturity that often results from a young man's basic military
training.

God created man with a free will. Therefore the parent should
not force the child's will but allow him to choose wrong or right,
while urging toward the better choice. The child will soon learn that
wrong choices bring consequences, including punishment, whereas
right choices bring blessings. Many times, just the absence of angry
conflict will itself prompt the child to choose right.

In most cases it is better to avoid a direct confrontation. In the
holy duty of training, both parent and child will grow together . . . *in
the unity of the faith, and of the knowledge of the Son of God, unto
a perfect man, unto the measure of the stature of the fulness of
Christ* . . . (Eph. 4:13).

A Charlotte Mason Companion

Karen Andreola
☞ ***Top 10 Book!***

A Charlotte Mason Companion provides a profusion of ideas on such
assorted topics as Shakespeare, Dickens, poetry, composition,
picture study, grammar, vocabulary, spelling, history, "bickerings"
and the effective and distinctive learning technique of *narration.*

✔ Read a paragraph or more of a good book. To encourage thought,
tell each child to consider what was particularly interesting or
notable about the passage. Then have each child, from the youngest

to the oldest, retell the material and include special details, while you write down their discourse. This will create a permanent record of your child's literacy and knowledge. When beginning, do this only once or twice a week. Karen also wisely suggests that the parent should listen attentively to the spontaneous narrations the child offers throughout the day.

Greek Myth & Fairy Tales

Charles Kingsley said, "There are no fairy tales like these old Greek ones for beauty, and wisdom, and truth, and for making children love noble deeds and [for encouraging] trust in God to help them through."[1]

Karen recommends Hawthorne's *Tanglewood Tales* and *The Wonder Book.* Charlotte Mason said, "Imagination grows by what it gets and the age of faith is the time for its nourishment. The children should have the joy of living in far lands, in other persons, in other times—in their storybooks." Charlotte suggested Andrew Lang's fairy tales. Author G.K. Chesterton said that fairy tales foster courage and truth more than any other literature and said of them:

> *We learn that the world is bound together in mysterious bonds of trust and compact precision and that even green dragons keep their promises. We learn that nothing is wasted in the mills of the world, that a jewel thrown into the sea, a kindness to a stricken bird, an idle word to a ragged wayfarer have in them some terrible value and are here bound up with the destiny of men.*

Nature Study

✔ Set aside a weekly day or half-day for your excursion. Record what you find: sketch and write about your specimen and your experience. Include the Latin name, if you can find it, along with poetry or a Bible verse. As you admire the Maker's works, remind your children to praise and thank Him.

The Country Diary of an Edwardian Lady, first published in 1906, is an example of a simple and lovely Charlotte Mason-style nature notebook. *Create Your Own Artist's Journal* by Erin O'Toole is another beautiful, newer book. Also see *Pocketful of Pinecones* by Karen Andreola and *Wild Days* by Karen Skidmore Rackliffe (reviews below). Read nature authors such as Ernest Seton-Thompson, Thornton Burgess and John Burroughs.

Bickerings

Gently draw the belligerent's mind to the fact that he is feeling very unhappy, that this is merely the natural result of saying unkind things and that, as it would not be fair to make everyone else unhappy too, he must go from the room till he can be pleasant.

✔ Help eliminate bickering by having your children confess their weakness to you. Then give them "weapons" for each day of the week—Bible verses focusing on that particular "giant." Have your child copy, memorize and recite his "weapon verses."

Enthusiasm

[Charlotte Mason] . . . wanted children to become acquainted with enthusiasm—heroes, and heroines, the poets, the prophets, the warriors, the high tempered spirits, the giants of human nature who through force of mind, courage and perseverance, have won the day for nations and also for individuals, when all other hearts but their own were faint, and who against all hope believed in hope, when others desponded. The enthusiast manifests a glowing splendor and gladness that leads him on to victory.
. . . Enthusiastic teachers press forward through difficulty and discouragement, knowing the sovereign power of love will not fail in the end. For love—the greatest thing in the world—can never fail.

The Successful Homeschool Family Handbook

Raymond and Dorothy Moore
☞ ***Top 10 Book!***

The Successful Homeschool Family Handbook not only arrests and stimulates, but also—more importantly—motivates to action. Be a loving, responsive parent. Respect your kids. Look forward to an abundant harvest. The Moore formula of education balances study, work and service. Use these pointers from the Moores in your homeschooling.

- The most important qualifications for homeschooling parents are warm responsiveness and a "fairly decent basic education."
- Allow the child time to pursue his interests, but do not eliminate all formal work.
- Do not school formally, especially boys, before the age of eight, and possibly even twelve, depending on their "IML" or Integrated Maturity Level. *This depends on the child. Because of this philosophy, I did not expect much from my sons. It was a mistake. I may have misinterpreted this advice, when it means more accurately, "Do not put your active son at a desk for six hours a day."*
- Read aloud and respond to your children from the earliest age. Younger children are well able to do narration and other effective learning activities. *I do not recommend busy-work for young children. It is best to read to them and encourage creative, independent play.*

> Expect the best from both your sons and your daughters.

- Rely on discussion and project learning, but also include drill as a tool for mastery of the basics.
- "If you want bright and balanced children, you must help them be thinkers, not mere reflectors of other's thoughts."
- Have fun with your children. "Warmly share your fellowship and sound example all day."
- Be extremely selective in choosing materials and workshops. Simplest materials and methods are best.

- Do not allow your children to spend more time with peers than parents. Doing so before age eleven or twelve causes peer dependency. *I've found that even older children can be negatively influenced by peers.*
- Children who feel needed, wanted and depended upon have the best self-confidence. The longer they are taught at home the higher this self-concept.
- Don't test unless required. Prepare if you must.
- Parents should exemplify a disciplined life before attempting to discipline their children.
- Encourage all good habits. Change the others, one at a time.
- Work on regularity and a flexible schedule.
- Demonstrate selfless, unconditional love.
- Teach service first at home, then elsewhere. Family industry and service are not electives. Share family management and family business. "Students who work with their hands develop common sense and practical skills and do much better with their heads."

Marva Collins' Way

Marva Collins and Civia Tamarkin
☞ ***Top 10 Book!***

With great literature and love Marva turned ghetto children around to self-respect and a love of learning. She tells her students on the first day of school:

> *I promise, you are going to do, you are going to produce. I am not going to let you fail. . . . Mrs. Collins is no miracle worker. I do not walk on water, I do not part the sea. I just love children and work harder than a lot of people and so will you. You will 1) read hard books and understand what you read, 2) write every day so that writing becomes second nature to you and 3) memorize a poem every week so that you can train your minds to remember things.*

Marva goes on to tell her students that success will not come to them but they will go to it, and that the first thing that they are going to do is a lot of believing in themselves.

Marva learned to read as her grandmother sounded out words from the Bible by syllables. Her introduction to literature was from that same Bible. Her grandmother also recited poems that she had learned as a girl, such as "Paul Revere's Ride" and "Hiawatha." Marva treasured books. She loved reading and read everything she could get her hands on. At age nine, she was thrilled with the words from Shakespeare, recited by her aunt, and read all of *Macbeth*.

> An error means that a child needs help, nothing more.

Her black family from Alabama was atypical for the time—they were affluent. Her father, a diligent businessman, was her greatest example. Marva taught for a short time at a trade school but claimed she knew nothing about educational theory. She believed that this was to her advantage.

Easy Ideas from Marva Collins

- Take a positive approach. Marva was constantly touching, hugging and complimenting her students.
- Display all papers.
- Do not mark papers with red but with "very good," "wonderful work" or a smiling face.
- When checking papers, take subtle notice of what needs teaching and teach as soon as possible.
- Use the blackboard or whiteboard.
- Stress proper speech and pronunciation.
- Have your children read aloud for pronunciation, comprehension and vocabulary building (stop them and ask the meaning).

Reading aloud helps your child realize the difference in punctuation usage and helps him read for ideas, not just words. Marva's students read everything aloud including their compositions. Thus, they became conscious of sentence structure and any needed changes and also developed presence and authority in front of an audience.

☞ Language Arts . . . the Easy Way

Cindy Rushton

Reading Cindy's writing is like getting refueled with premium gasoline and plenty of it! *Language Arts . . . the Easy Way* is packed with tips, encouragement and ideas. This book gives details for writing class; explains the process of learning; suggests whole books; covers teaching subjects using whole books, copywork and narration; tells of Charlotte Mason's dictation class; has instructions for "binderizing" (using notebooks) and scrapbooking. Moreover Cindy's writing motivates all-important change.

Hints from Cindy Rushton

- Help your children find reasons for writing.
- Require them to write.
- Read voraciously.
- Use narration.
- Do not accept sloppy work.
- Dictate only when your child is familiar with the passage.
- Read whole books.
- Keep books accessible.
- Use the Bible.
- Read lots of biographies.
- Use copywork.
- Use notebooks.

☞ The Real Life Homeschool Mom

Virginia Knowles

I began reading Virginia's book when we were in a family crisis. As the situation weighed heavily on my heart, Virginia's scripture-filled book began lifting it off. *Real Life . . .* meets real needs head on. It brought me to tears and to the foot of the Headmaster. It reminded me that we should "see circumstances through God's eyes." Virginia transparently shares from her heart that moms in leadership have similar feelings, needs and circumstances as those that aren't. (No, we haven't arrived. In fact, some of you have probably surpassed us!)

Virginia gleans from all methods but says she leans toward unit studies. There are topics in the book that were not of interest to me, but then it covers just about everything—pregnancy, newborns, husbands, support networks, abiding in Christ and homeschooling theory. Virginia includes Bible verse lists for theme studies. Scriptures, when used, are from the *New International Version.* The following is adapted and condensed from Virginia's jam-packed book.

Eight Essentials from Virginia

1) Determine style and capabilities of each child.
2) Write goals, set up routines, assign work.
3) Provide appropriate tools.
4) Clearly demonstrate how to do each task.
5) Add a little adventure.
6) Develop a sense of teamwork.
7) Evaluate success.
8) Encourage an attitude of excellence.

Raising a Modern Day Knight

Robert Lewis

When does a boy become a man? This question motivated pastor and father Robert Lewis to seek an answer. What he found from history, God's word and the example of Christ was that a real man is one who 1) rejects passivity, 2) accepts responsibility, 3) leads courageously and 4) expects a greater reward.

Lewis says that a man will either be like Adam or like Christ. Adam was passive regarding temptation, instead of protective and assertive. Today we see multiplied examples of the inferior manhood of Adam.

Jesus is the perfect example of manhood. He lived a life in union with God and had direction, faith, elevated masculinity and a generous rather than a selfish life. Robert Lewis calls the Bible, the "Knight's Handbook." Consider these knightly characteristics.

- Loyalty: *Hos. 6:6*
- Servant Leadership: *Luke 22:26*
- Kindness: *Prov. 19:22*
- Humility: *Phil. 2*
- Purity: *1 Tim. 4:12*
- Honesty: *Eph. 4*
- Self Discipline: *1 Tim. 4*
- Excellence: *1 Cor. 9:24*
- Integrity: *Prov. 10:9*
- Perseverance: *Gal. 4*

A young man is trained to knighthood by the godly example of his father. The father can point out Biblical applications from the lives of others or from world or local events. (Deut. 6:6-7) The father can inspire through stories. When our children were small, my husband did one-man Bible shows for them and other visiting children, using props and "costumes" he brought from all corners of our house.

A godly father helps his son find a mission in life, his spiritual gifts and his ministry. A knight needs to be taught to honor women and be ready to aid them. Men are called by God to love, lead and honor their wives. This book deserves close study and application by the father *and* the mother! Scripture references are from the *New International Version*.

Wild Days

Karen Skidmore Rackliffe

It was a perfect fall day. I sat on our porch in the morning quiet while birds sang and the train softly whistled miles away. It was a perfect day for reading *Wild Days*. *Wild Days* is a practical guide and is charmingly illustrated with the writer's family's works and some photos too. Karen Skidmore Rackliffe begins her book by saying:

> *When the days are wild, I grab a journal and pen and head out the door. I leave behind the phones and buzzers, beeps and lists . . . . So, we go to some wild place to watch the clouds, the river, the birds, the blossoms, the wildlife. It's like coming home . . . .*

Karen's son, Isaac, eleven, gives us these tips for the nature sketchbooks: "You should put the dates and label what you saw and tell something you know about it. It helps you to remember the day." Anita, fourteen, lyrically relates:

> *Nature is the breath of life. It has a strong sense of peace and joy. It is a place where you can think, a place to unload your troubles. A place that is close to God. A place that is necessary for everyone's mental, spiritual and emotional health.*

Wild Days will not only motivate you to get out of your house, it provides instruction and suggests materials.

Pocketful of Pinecones

Karen Andreola

With some books reading is a chore. I abhor the clutter of unnecessary words, repetitive phrases and even paragraphs that waste my time and only distract from an important message. Too many words in too many works, both old and new, seem to have been written just to fill the page—and perhaps the pocketbook. I will not waste my time on a book like that, but when I find a book that is concise as well as interesting, it is refreshing and keeps me reading. *Pocketful of Pinecones* is one of those books. Although *Pocketful of Pinecones* is the fictional account of Carol, a mother living in the 1930s, the book is based on Karen Andreola's experiences with her own children. The book highlights Charlotte Mason's nature study methods.

Karen's gentleness is evident as she writes of the decisions Carol makes as she balances life's demands. Carol gives careful attention to her words. She thinks before speaking so as not to be harsh to her family. Carol speaks wisely of gentle learning:

> *Not all of what they will learn about God's creation will conveniently fit into my lessons. My students have a lifetime ahead of them in which to observe and discover—to become self-educated in their leisure, so to speak. My job is to allow their feet to walk the paths of wonder, to see that they form relations to various things, so that when the habit is formed, they will carry an appreciation for nature with them throughout their lives.*

Pocketful of Pinecones leads toward more gentle motherhood and even toward humility before one's husband. It inspires thoughts God-ward with poems, hymn lyrics and the lifestyle portrayed.

> *My devotions gave the day its energy. . . . It is proof that I remember Him, depend on His mercy, which is so thankfully new every morning. It is evidence that I trust Him. It is because my days are so busy that I have kept myself*

*from the God-can-wait syndrome. I need my heavenly
Father and so I seek Him early. Prayers are the wings of
the soul. They bear the Christian far from earth, out of its
cares, its woes and its perplexities, into glorious serenity. It
is the first God-ward step that the soul takes.*

This book would be an especially appropriate gift for a new mother,
a young mother or someone contemplating homeschooling. It gives
a gentle introduction to easy methods through Carol's example. It
was written simply, for the busy mother, making it appropriate to
read to the youngest child. Karen includes recommended resources
and excerpts from Charlotte Mason's book, *Home Education.*
Pocketful of Pinecones is a book that you will continue to pick up
until you have reached the last pages that tell of the Andreolas' life
in Maine.

☞ Home School, High School, and Beyond . . .
Beverly L. Adams-Gordon

Although a student's book, Beverly Adams-Gordon suggests that a
parent read *Home School, High School, and Beyond . . .* first. It is
full of information for those embarking on high school, including
ideas for ❀ **goal setting,** planning individual courses, completing
projects and courses and preparing for tests. *Home School, High
School, and Beyond . . .* could be used as a framework for any
number of creative high school options.

Home School, High School, and Beyond . . . motivated Jessica
to check out books from the library on careers and planning. I
disagree with the emphasis on new books, but would use old books
and reap old-fashioned, well-educated young adults.

✔ For current information in fields such as science and government,
use alternate sources, such as current magazines.

Review by Jessica J. Curry

> Ask God what He wants to do in your life. If you don't do this now you may have to start again from the very beginning in your thirties.
>
> *Jessica Curry*

Home School, High School, and Beyond . . . *tells how high schoolers should keep records (it includes all the necessary forms), pray for guidance in choosing a career and make sure to plan well (otherwise it will cost you time and money). The author says you must be meticulous in your record- keeping, do everything record-wise correctly or you will reap the sad rewards in your last year in high school. Which are, by the way, having to go back and sort everything you did in high school into the proper organization and having to go back and take classes you missed that you need for credits.*

You should ask God what He wants to do in your life. If you don't do this now you may have to start again from the very beginning in your thirties.

Plan well and get the material you need, including up-to-date textbooks and encyclopedias. If you use old books you won't get into college—colleges want up-to-date students, not ones who know what the latest fashion was in the 1800s. In other words, you can read old books like encyclopedias and novels but don't expect to get into college—or get high school credits—using old information and antique textbooks.

Be prepared, do everything correctly and don't forget record-keeping. If you do all that, you should make it happily through high school and college.

The SAT & College Preparation Book for the Christian Student

James Stobaugh

James Stobaugh is a homeschooling father, pastor, secondary teacher and SAT coach. His focus in this book is spiritual preparation for the SAT. The daily worksheets (already punched to put in a notebook) begin with a scripture or quote, a devotional and include thought-provoking questions along with a sampling of math problems. In the back of the book, Dr. Stobaugh provides a booklist, a list of possible target scriptures, test-taking tips, math answers and a bibliography that lists other helpful SAT books. Also provided are two reproducible worksheets:

> Protagonist:
> *the principal character in a literary work*
>
> Antagonist:
> *one that contends with or opposes another*
>
> *www.m-w.com*

1) The "Thirty Minute Prayer Devotional" gives guidelines for focusing, reading and meditating on Scripture and praying. It includes questions to answer.

2) The "Reading Journal" asks the student to briefly describe protagonist and antagonist, compare the book's characters with Bible characters and share world view.

✔ Learn five new vocabulary words each week. Select words from the book your child is reading that week, or from your read-aloud book. Write a word on one side of an index card. Write the definition and a sentence using the word on the other side. Repeat for the other four words. Review these vocabulary cards regularly.

America's God and Country
William J. Federer

America's God and Country is an encyclopedia of quotations highlighting the godly heritage of the United States. The quotations are those of Americans, as well as of other well-known people such as composers and scientists. Faith, character and sometimes sparkling personality are communicated through their words. Here are ideas for using this extraordinary resource.

- Dictate passages to your student.
- Have your student copy or memorize selections.
- Use *America's God and Country* as a supplement to a textbook.
- Use this work for other studies, by looking up the quotations of the scientist, artist or composer you are reading about.
- Use this book for your American history curriculum, following a time line or other guide. Look up each individual as they "appeared" in history. You could do additional research on persons or events of interest.
- Just read it, as I did, cover to cover. You will be so uplifted! This is one book that will leave you hopeful.

☞ God and Government
Gary DeMar

God and Government is a superb three-volume set that emphasizes government in light of the Word of God. *God and Government* includes numerous scriptures, notes, references and questions that will engage your pupil's brain. It is perfect for young adults because it begins with the government of the individual (self-government) and family government, leaving no doubt in the student's mind why and to whom they are to submit. ❀ **Just add believing prayer to transfer submission to their hearts!**

Whatever Happened to Justice?
Richard J. Maybury

We started reading this when my children were ages ten to fifteen. I loved every word of it but in the midst of my own serious freedom fight, I was disappointed that I found no hopeful ending—no steps to take to right the wrongs. *Whatever Happened to Justice?* provides abundant information and is written in a simple-to-understand manner. Maybury says that all people can agree on the two fundamental laws.

1) Do all you have agreed to do.

2) Do not encroach on other persons or their property.

Political Law
Zephi Curry, 13

Political law is the type of law that we have today. It is created out of nothing, is based upon brutal force, not on the two fundamental laws. Political law is vulgar and uncouth, has no requirement for logic or morality, and is unreasonable. You must do what the power holders say, or else.

Common Law
Jessica Curry, 15

Political law should be abolished and Common Law reintroduced to America's government. For truly, this was the foundation upon which our government was laid. Political law has stopped America in her tracks. She is at a standstill because her pores are clogged with political law. She is bursting at the seams with political law! Political law has hurt her badly. The author of Whatever Happened to Justice? *firmly believes that we must return to Common Law, the foundations of which are the two fundamental laws.*

Maybury includes a list of movies to spark discussion about law but we were not able to find many at the library. I didn't like the "Uncle Eric" letter format and eliminated that when I read it aloud.

Do we really need to study law? Our country's founders would probably say it's no wonder we've floundered. In their day almost everyone studied it.

✍ Uncle Tom's Cabin; or, Life Among The Lowly
Harriet Beecher Stowe

This book made people so aware of the slave's plight that even Lincoln said that it was the catalyst for the great Civil War. It was immensely popular in its time, selling into the millions—3,000 on its first day of publication. I am amazed that this book (one fragile copy) was on our library shelves. The text includes racial stereotypes, the use of the word "nigger" and portrayal of Christian lifestyles. This great book could be a lifetime vocabulary lesson, while passages are descriptive and touching. It certainly awakens sympathy for the heavy burdens these people experienced and for those, including the pre-born, who are brutalized today. Mrs. Stowe said of her book:

> *God wrote it. I merely did His dictation. . . . The object of these sketches is to awaken sympathy and feeling for the African race, as they exist among us . . . to show their wrongs and sorrows, under a system so necessarily cruel and unjust as to defeat and do away the good effects of all that can be attempted for them. . . .*

Mothering

Rachel moved gently and quietly about, making biscuits, cutting up chicken, and diffusing a sort of sunny radiance over the whole proceeding generally. If there was any danger of friction or collision from the ill-regulated zeal of so many young operators, her gentle "Come, come!" or "I

*wouldn't, now," was quite sufficient to allay the diffi-
culty. . . . Rachel never looked so truly and benignly happy
as at the head of her table. There was so much motherliness
and full-heartedness even in the way she passed a plate of
cakes or poured a cup of coffee, that it seemed to put a
spirit into the food and drink she offered. . . .*

A Christian Family

*This indeed was a home,—home—a word that George had
never yet known a meaning for; and a belief in God, and
trust in His providence, began to encircle his heart, as with
a golden cloud of protection and confidence. . . . preached
by a thousand unconscious acts of love and good will. . . .*

Bible Study

*As for Tom's Bible. . . he would designate by bold, strong
marks and dashes, with pen and ink, the passages which
more particularly gratified his ear or affected his
heart. . . .and while it lay there before him, every passage
breathing of some old home scene, and recalling some past
enjoyment, his Bible seemed to him all of this life that
remained as well as the promise of a future one.*

To Be A Slave
Julius Lester

A book of vignettes—the slaves' own words about their experiences.
I skipped over the few sentences that mention nudity. This is one of
the advantages of reading aloud.

Red Badge of Courage
Stephen Crane

A realistic, well written, portrayal of a young man's journey from cowardice to courage through his experiences in the Civil War. Descriptions of the results of fear and valor have Biblical parallels.

Great Speeches
Abraham Lincoln

This book includes the great man's actual words from the time he was an attorney until after the war. "If destruction be our lot, we must ourselves be its author and finisher. As a nation of freemen, we must live through all time, or die by suicide."

Behind The Blue And The Gray
Delia Ray

The soldier's life in the civil war, including details and quotes.

Stonewall Jackson
Dr. Robert Lewis Dabney
Excerpt from—Dabney's Discussions Vol. IV

Dabney's *Life of Stonewall Jackson* is on the Robinson Curriculum list. This is not that book, but the text of a lecture on Jackson's life given in November of 1872. It covers a portion of the time Dabney spent on Jackson's staff and includes battle details. Also in the booklet is a sermon that Rev. Dabney delivered at Jackson's memorial service on the first Sabbath of June 1863 before a vast assemblage of officers, soldiers and citizens. (Jackson died on May 10th.) The title of this eulogy is "True Courage."

According to Dabney, there are three types of courage: 1) animal, which is characterized by "irrational thoughtlessness," 2) the courage that seeks applause and is motivated by pride, and 3) true courage:

*The third species is the moral courage of him who fears
God, and, for that reason, fears nothing else. There is an
intelligent apprehension of danger; there is the natural
instinct of self-love desiring to preserve its own well-being;
but it is curbed and governed by the sense of duty, and
desire for the approbation of God. This alone is true courage; true virtue; for it is rational, and its motive is moral
and unselfish. It is a true Christian grace, when found in its
purest forms, a grace whose highest exemplar, and whose
source is the Divine Redeemer; whose principle is that
parent grace of soul faith.* David and Samuel and the
prophets, through faith subdued kingdoms . . . waxed
valiant in fight, turned to flight the armies of the
aliens. . . *(Heb. 11:33, 34).*

The Hiding Place

Corrie ten Boom, John and Elizabeth Sherrill

Heroic and impressive in content, *The Hiding Place* is a "Christian
Colossus," as is the older, *Uncle Tom's Cabin.* Miss ten Boom and
her family dared to help the Jews during WW
II, resulting in her family's arrest, imprison-
ment and mistreatment by the Germans. *The
Hiding Place* portrays the evil of the Nazi
regime, which was definitely demonic with
ghastly sins against man and God and even
special punishment for having a Bible.

> God always
> sustains and
> provides for
> those who
> trust in Him.

    This book is a testimony of God's
keeping power. In deepest needs—even when
help is not humanly possible, God sustains and provides. This is a
thought-provoking spiritual giant of a book. *The Hiding Place* is
dense with teaching, cover-to-cover; it is riveting, cover-to-cover; it
is Christian, cover-to-cover.

    I probably would not read this book aloud if my children were
very young, and yet reading it is much less startling than seeing the
movie. My boys (ages nine and ten) could not picture the horror of

the concentration camp, so I showed them a library book with a picture of the emaciated men three bunks high and more hesitatingly, a picture of a young German boy walking by many bodies.

Never Give In

Stephen Mansfield

Winston Churchill was one of the few real modern-day heroes. His faith and courage against Hitler's advances kept the world from certain and total horror.

> *Never Give In* reveals more than superficial facts and events.

I was anxious to read this book after reading several of Churchill's quotes. Since we were also reading the spellbinding book, *The Hiding Place*, the first few basic biographical chapters seemed exceedingly bland. What I did like about this book was that the middle chapters were titled with character traits, each one detailing how Churchill exemplified that trait.

One of the purposes of *Never Give In* was to prove that Churchill was a Christian. I wasn't convinced. However, even many Christians today fall far short of his high and righteous life principles. I loved him for these. I also identified with him because I was involved in my own "war" for my mother's freedom and Constitutional rights. Churchill encouraged me with his words, "Never give in, never give in, never, never, never, never—in nothing, great or small, large or petty—never give in, except to convictions of honor and good sense."

This "Leaders in Action" book—by looking at home life, education, character traits, faith and more—thoroughly explores what made Winston S. Churchill great. Thus it provides a much-needed "living" example of a real hero for our children. I recommend it. I also like the many quotes, for nothing reveals a personality better than a man's own words.

✍ In the Reign of Terror
G. A. Henty

Review by Jessica J. Curry, age fifteen.

This book gives a fine example of a boy's courage, selflessness, love and devotion to a just cause. Harry Sandwith, sixteen, was sent to France from England to be a companion to an aristocrat's son. He becomes part of the family after saving two of its sisters from a mad dog and a son from a "demon" wolf.

In Paris, the Reign of Terror escalates and the baron and his wife go to stand by the king and queen. The children soon follow. As events transpire, the baron and his wife are murdered, the two brothers try to escape (only to be killed near the border) and Harry takes it upon himself to get the three sisters to England. After leaving the eldest with her fiance, Harry—through many trials and troubles—attempts to get Jeanne and Anne Marie to England. Harry proposes to Jeanne near journey's end and she accepts. They all finally make it safe and sound back home to Harry's parents' home. This book reminds me of "The Scarlet Pimpernel" novel, *Eldorado,* because much of the plot is the same.

✍ Try and Trust
Horatio Alger, Jr.

Review by Ezra Curry, age twelve.

An old man and a young lad were traveling together. The burglar was following them and he had a beard. They stopped at an inn and this room had two beds—one bigger in the corner and one smaller. The young lad said that the old man could have the big bed. So they sat down and the old guy pulled a package out of his carpet bag and said that it was several thousand dollars. As they were talking about guns, the young lad said that he'd keep his loaded and ready. The old guy said, "You know how to load a gun?" The old man put the package of money under the mattress.

Then the robber put a ladder up and crept up the ladder and slowly opened the window. The young lad jumped out of bed quietly (he had slept in his trousers in case of an emergency). He hid with his gun ready.

The robber was starting to get ready to climb in the window when the young lad stepped out and said, "Get down or I'll shoot."

> I don't want to kill him and I really don't want to hurt him. I'll shoot the first round in the air and then if that doesn't scare him off, I'll wound him.

The robber said, "You wouldn't dare and when I get in there, I'll give you something to remember me by." So the young lad fired one round in the air. Then the robber said, "Please don't shoot me and I'll give you some of it." Then the robber saw the carpet bag and started to get it. The boy fired a shot in his shoulder and he fell to the ground with a thud.

Then there was a knock on his door and he opened it and there were a lot of people there from the inn. They said, "What's going on up here?" The young lad said, "Come here to the window and I will show you." They saw the robber on the ground moaning with pain. They said, "Brave young lad!" They lit a lantern and the lad said, "He's in pain, we should help him." The innkeeper said, "Naw . . . he deserves it!" Then the old man said, "Bring him in and I'll pay for the room." The innkeeper said, "I really don't want to, but I have to." They brought him in and got a doctor. Then the boy was talking to the robber and the robber said, "You're the boy that shot me. I curse you!"

So the rich man gave him some of the money because he was so brave. He got a job at a counting room and the other boys his age were not getting as much pay as he did because he was the best worker. The other people thought he was a thief because he was so rich but he was richer than the other people because he was so famous. Then in the end, he paid off the mortgages on his house. I didn't like the beginning and the end as much as the middle of the book because it was more interesting.

✍ Phil the Fiddler

Horatio Alger, Jr.

Review by Zephi Curry, age fourteen.

Phil the Fiddler is a book about a small, twelve-year-old Italian boy named Filippo (Phil) whose father "leased" him to a padrone in the city of New York. The father did it because he was short on money. Phil was a naturally "merry and light-hearted" boy and had an olive complexion. He had a friend called Giacomo. Giacomo was "leased" to the padrone and had been friends with Filippo almost from infancy—they had grown up with each other in the same town in Italy.

The book tells about how Phil has to go to work every day in the streets, playing his violin for people and taking up a collection afterwards. He starts early in the morning and works until about 11:00 p.m. at night. He had to take at least two dollars back to the padrone at night or else he would be beaten severely and sent to bed with no supper. Usually all he gets to eat is bread and cheese at each meal of breakfast, dinner and supper, unless someone gives him something else, like an apple.

Then one day this gentleman that he met in a grocery store gave him the idea of running away from the padrone. This idea got bigger and bigger in Phil's mind and then after Giacomo falls sick, Phil decides to escape. All along, Filippo knows full well what's to come, should he run away. The padrone would send his nephew and able assistant, Peitro, to find him and bring him back. If the escapee was found, he'd get punished worse than usual, but Phil's American friend helps him get to Jersey City.

In the end, Peitro and his uncle do not catch Filippo. The padrone went to jail for something else and Peitro becomes the next child-abusing padrone.

> A small, 12-year-old Italian boy named Filippo (Phil) was "leased" by his father to a padrone in the city of New York.

Do you want to find out how Phil grows up? Read the book! It has a great ending that I'm not going to tell you about. Part of this book is even hilarious!

8

Loving Literature

any ☞ **Exceptional Books** have passed through my fingers throughout the years, yet I hold tightly to volumes of poems and quotations that rejoice, uplift and calm the spirit, and literature texts with exquisite excerpts and brilliant biographies. When I have had a long fast from a great novel, I find myself longing for the day when I will again lose myself in one. I love literature—but then, literature is not difficult to love. This makes it an ideal tool for homeschooling.

> *From the total training during childhood there should result in the child a taste for interesting and improved reading, which should direct and inspire its subsequent intellectual life. The schooling which results in this taste for good reading, however unsystematic or eccentric the schooling may have been, has achieved a main end of elementary education; and that schooling which does not result in implanting this permanent taste has failed.*[1]

Literature-based learning is distinctive for several reasons. Reading stimulates brain development. As the brain works to comprehend, it is exercised and actually branches.[2] Then the student becomes educated as facts and ideas are absorbed from the content. Most importantly, true literature elevates the spirit of man, refining thought, character and emotions. It gives us hope, love, appreciation, consolation for our failures, rebuke for our vices and suggestions for our ambition. It encourages us to constructive and positive action, attitudes and manners. "As a tree is judged by its fruits, so is literature judged . . . by the effect which it produces on human life. . . ."[3] Has the book elicited tears or laughter? Can one identify with the characters' emotions or viewpoint, especially with their faith? Characters in true literature can be admired and imitated. If a book has lived from generation to generation, it is because of these qualities. If it has evoked similar sympathies from generations far removed from each other, it is a great book. "If your book has not taught you . . . some practical lesson for life, or awakened pure thoughts, or stimulated noble actions and appealed to heightened motives, your time is then worse than wasted."[4]

Eternal Qualities

[Great literature] . . .deals with common experiences of joy or sorrow, pain or pleasure that all men understand; it cherishes the unchanging ideals of love, faith, duty, freedom, reverence, courtesy . . . . Therefore are great books characterized by lofty thoughts, by fine feeling and as a rule, by a beautiful simplicity of expression. They have another quality, hard to define but easy to understand, a quality which leaves upon us the impression of eternal youth.[5]

Literature is a record of man's "best thought and feeling."[6] Even if written hundreds of years ago, such literature continues to have the quality of "eternal youth" because the emotions and thoughts expressed in the work are eternal. We identify with these common— yet God-made—qualities because we are eternal beings. This common thread makes the books "living" and their authors our contemporaries no matter when they lived. "The only valuable or interesting feature of any work of literature is its vitality."[7]

English and American Literature

Literature . . . is the reflection and the reproduction of the life of the people. . . . Greek literature tells us how the Greeks lived and how they felt, what they thought and what they did. . . . In a like manner, English literature tells us about the life of the peoples who speak the English language. English literature is the record of the thoughts and the feelings and the acts of the great English-speaking race.[8]

We English-speaking Christians should major in English and American literature because it is Christian: it portrays our Christian culture—the most emulated, prosperous and successful culture of history, and very worthy of our study.

It is unfortunate that our current culture has been tainted with debased and debasing writings. Literature—and today, television—shapes a nation by shaping the thoughts of the individuals of that nation. This makes it imperative that our children are protected from evil at every age and then provided with the most noble literature. (2 Cor. 6:17)

The Author

Literature magnifies the writer—his or her character, nationality and passions. The best literature for a Christian is that written by a Christian, or at least by an author with a Christian or Biblical worldview.

It would take a book to list suitable authors. I have one planned. In the meantime, consider Americans such as Benjamin Franklin, Washington Irving, William Cullen Bryant, Henry Wadsworth Longfellow, Nathaniel Hawthorne, John Greenleaf Whittier, Ralph Waldo Emerson, Oliver Wendell Holmes, James Russell Lowell, Henry David Thoreau and Mark Twain.

Some well-known British authors are Shakespeare, John Milton and the poet, Edmund Spenser. His work, *The Faerie Queene* (1590) was written to inspire men and boys to greatness. In it, knights represent virtues such as holiness, temperance, charity, friendship, justice and courtesy and fight their opposing vices. Written in Early Middle English, the primary difference from today's language is the spelling.

The Red Cross Knight

And on his brest a bloodie cross he bore,
The deare remembrance of his dying Lord,
For whose sweet sake, that glorious badge he wore.[9]

✔ Copy a portion of *The Faerie Queen* and and use your spell checker to rewrite into a work much easier to comprehend. Search at **www.google.com** or at **www.uoregon.edu/~rbear/ queene4.html**

Other British Authors

It was said of essayist and hymn writer, Joseph Addison (1672-1719), that ". . . his pen did much more than the pulpit to civilize the age and make virtue the fashion."[10]

John Ruskin (1819-1900) was an art critic, nature lover and philanthropist who turned man's thoughts heavenward as he brought spiritual and moral meaning into his deeply descriptive and lovely writings. For exciting and detailed history, read Thomas Carlyle's (1795-1881) *The French Revolution* (1837). Other notable authors are Charles Dickens, Robert Louis Stevenson, Jane Austen and the Brontë Sisters—Charlotte, Anne and Emily.

Charlotte Bronte & *Jane Eyre*

The Brontë children associated with their elders exclusively, read a great deal, and had a intelligent grasp of world affairs. After their mother died, the Brontë sisters spent a short time at boarding school and then studied under their Aunt Elizabeth. During this time, they wrote many booklets of stories, verses and essays—in the minutest handwriting. Charlotte came home at sixteen to share her increased learning in French, composition and drawing with her younger siblings.

> Doctrines should not be substituted for the world redeeming creed of Christ.
>
> *C. Brontë*

In *Jane Eyre,* the curtain opens upon the cruel treatment Jane is receiving from the son of her caretakers. She was then placed in an institutional boarding school by her aunt who hated her. (Scenes and passages in the book are based on Charlotte's own harsh experiences.)

Jane Eyre depicts demonic possession (labeled as madness) and romance—yet this is lofty and pure romance, not the sensuality that society defines as romance in our day. However, it was controversial in its day, because the man that Jane cared about was married, albeit to an insane woman. Jane flees temptation and suffers great hardship, but is eventually blessed for it with her heart's desire.

Miss Brontë's characters encourage Christian virtues in duress and speak of the ways of the Master. That Charlotte Brontë was a true Christian writer is disclosed in her preface to the third edition of *Jane Eyre* (October, 1847).

> *Appearance should not be mistaken for truth; narrow human doctrines, that only tend to elate and magnify a few, should not be substituted for the world-redeeming creed of Christ. There is—I repeat it—a difference; and it is a good and not a bad action to mark broadly and clearly the line of separation between them.*

Jane Eyre is realistic and intense. The main plot and sub-plots are interwoven to keep one reading "just one more chapter." This book fulfills many of the requirements that make great literature. A steady diet of such literature will have one speaking and writing beautifully.

Jane Austen

Jane Austen, the daughter of a clergyman and product of a happy home, was bright, beautiful, witty and cheerful.[11] There was great emphasis on propriety and manners in the Austen home, although Jane was no stranger to menial household duties. Hers was the simple country life and this life became the setting for her novels. Miss Austen wrote of what she knew best. She excelled in examining the human nature of those around her, thus her novels examine clergy, old maids, mothers and young women available for marriage. Jane's rule of writing was *edit much,* which produced a finished style.

> Jane's care in editing produced a finished style.

"Copy-books from her fourteenth year, containing sketches and stories which precociously shadow forth the splendid vein of irony she was later to develop, are most remarkable in the sure critical sense which they display."[12] "Her satire is perhaps the best that has been written . . . so delicate, so flashing, so keen."[13]

Miss Austen's works are no great moral treatises but merely give a picture of life in Victorian times—swooning, smelling salts, family entertainment, well-fitted parlors, estates and so on. They portray light romance with examples of courtship: a beau is usually known by the family (sometimes even part of the family, perhaps a cousin) with the chaperone most often being an older sibling. In my opinion, Austen's books are best viewed as leisure reading although they can be studied for writing style and proper usage of English.

Although *Pride and Prejudice* is her most popular book, it is not considered to be her best. Better are *Emma, Sense and Sensibility, Persuasion* and *Northanger Abbey.*

Jane Austen's Works
By Jennifer Robinson
Home school graduate, writing and editing since age 13.

Jane Austen, an English writer considered by some to be the greatest female novelist, is admired most for her sharp wit, keen insight and charming literary style. She published six novels—*Pride and Prejudice, Sense and Sensibility, Emma, Mansfield Park, Northanger Abbey* and *Persuasion*—whose main themes are the manner in which the heroine and her family react to society's moral standards and traditional class structure.

Pride and Prejudice is a romantic comedy that tells the story of the tenacious Elizabeth Bennet. Known as Lizzy to family and close friends, she was born the second of five daughters. The arrival to the neighborhood of two wealthy young bachelors, Mr. Bingley and his friend Mr. Darcy, incites Mrs. Bennet's quest to marry off her daughters. Through the course of events, Lizzy realizes it is best not to judge someone's character too quickly. (John 7:24, Matt. 7:1-5)

> Jane Austen's charming writings are known for sharp wit and keen insight.

Sense and Sensibility centers on the lives of two sisters who are completely opposite in personality. Elinor Dashwood is the practical older sister, while Marianne is outwardly passionate and tends to take her romantic sensibilities too far. Impoverished when the family estate is left to a stepbrother, their hopes of marrying well become almost nonexistent. Elinor must hide her affection for the steady Mr. Ferrars because he is engaged to another woman. Marianne's infatuation with the dashing Mr. Willoughby almost causes her to forfeit the opportunity to have genuine love. Their situations were different, but Elinor and Marianne learn the value of balancing emotion with reason. (Proverbs 1:2-5)

Emma is the tale of the charming and clever Miss Woodhouse, whose desire to help the people around her is occasionally overshadowed by her misdirected actions. Emma determines to help an orphan named Harriet to be respectable in society in order to increase her prospects of a good marriage. She learns a difficult lesson when her good intentions cause her more grief than happiness; in the process, she grows into a mature young woman.

Mansfield Park tells the story of a very different heroine. Shy, timid, and seemingly uninteresting, Fanny Price is taken from her impoverished home to live with wealthy relatives when very young. She is treated as an inferior, but eventually gains the respect and affection of her patrons. Fanny's story is about the difference between appearances and reality.

Northanger Abbey depicts a very imaginative, but naïve heroine. In the story, Catherine Morland visits a resort in Bath with friends. While there she is invited to stay with a family, whose home is a medieval abbey. An avid reader of gothic-style horror novels, she becomes obsessed with the mystery surrounding the abbey. Her imagination runs wild until she is confronted with the danger of confusing real life with fantasy.

Persuasion was Jane Austen's final novel. It is the account of Anne Elliot, an intelligent woman who is disregarded by her family and social circle because of a previous engagement. The man, considered beneath her in status, is a young naval officer named Captain Wentworth. Many years later they meet again, and must decide if they will forgive and offer each other a second chance.

The stories Jane Austen wrote were genuine. She had a gift for making her characters real; the reader can identify with their strengths and weaknesses. Today, her work is still appreciated for the poignant way she portrayed the struggles and triumphs in matters of the heart.

Expression and the Bible

Literature is not merely words or thoughts, but is distinguished by the manner of expression the author has used. This manner of expression or style exhibits the author's creativity and shows itself in the musical flow of words, the aptness and grace of the images, the elimination of unnecessary words and phrases and the refinement of those that are left.[14]

> A child might receive a liberal education from the Bible alone.
>
> *C. Mason*

The pinnacle of expression in literature can be found in The Authorized King James Bible. "It is impossible to estimate the influence which this 'Authorized Version' has had on the language and literature of the English race."[15]

The great educator Charlotte Mason had much wisdom to impart about the use of the Bible as literature, for schooling and as a character training tool. Her comments here are extracted from *The Original Home Schooling Series.*

- *The habit of hearing, and later, of reading the Bible, is one to establish at an early age.* (Vol. 3, p. 142)

- *What is required of us is that we should implant a love of the Word; that the most delightful moments of the child's day should be those in which his mother reads for him . . . the beautiful stories of the Bible.* (Vol. 1, p. 349)

- *It is a mistake to use paraphrases of the text; the fine roll of Bible English appeals to children with a compelling music, and they will probably retain through life their first conception of Bible scenes and also, the very words in which these scenes are portrayed.* (Vol. 1, p. 249)

- *For Religion it is, no doubt, to the Bible itself we must go, as the great storehouse of spiritual truth and moral impressions. A child might, in fact, receive a liberal education from the Bible alone, for "The Book" contains within itself a great literature.* (Vol. 3, p. 235)

- *The Bible is not a single book, but a classic literature of wonderful beauty and interest; that, apart from its Divine sanc-*

tions and religious teaching, from all that we understand by revelation, the Bible, as a mere instrument of education, is, at the least, as valuable as the classics of Greece or Rome. . . . All the literatures of the world put together utterly fail to give us a system of ethics, in precept and example, motive and sanction, complete as that to which we have been born as our common inheritance in the Bible. (Vol. 2, p. 104)

Poetry

> The sunlight clasps the earth, and the moonbeams kiss the sea; what are all these kissings worth, if thou kiss not me?
>
> *Shelley*

Poetry is the loftiest form of literature. It is created to express the deepest emotions and crafted to express them lyrically with carefully chosen words. Some of the more common sentiments of poetry are love of nature and nature's God, love of family, brave deeds, patriotism and romantic love.

Poetry has the innate power to slow us down, as we pause and meditate on what the words are saying to us. We can think of poetry as tea time—a much needed break in our harried lifestyles.

Come read to me some poem
Some simple and heartfelt lay,
That shall sooth the restless feeling,
And banish the thoughts of the day. . . .

Then read from the treasured volume
The poem of thy choice,
And lend to the rhyme of the poet
The beauty of thy voice. . . .

Longfellow, "The Day is Done"

The Poet

No matter how many decades or centuries have past, we can know the poet well by knowing his writing. We will be most drawn to those poets with whom we share values, feelings and faith. With some poets—such as John Greenleaf Whittier—we become morally inspired. His poems breathe courage and duty to the inner "man," even in the face of mighty obstacles. Other great poets inspire reverence for God even when displaying a minute observation in nature.

We are not only moved by the imagery of poetry, but by clear language. Lyrical flow makes the reader feel more strongly what the poet is expressing. Truth is expressed with Beauty and together they breathe Purity. The greatest poetry is deeply spiritual. "Unexpectedly almost we find ourselves in the presence of Divinity itself and the humblest meets the loftiest on common ground."[16]

> *And I have felt*
> *A presence that disturbs me with the joy*
> *Of elevated thoughts; a sense sublime*
> *Of something far more deeply interfused,*
> *Whose dwelling is the light of setting suns,*
> *And the round ocean, and the living air,*
> *And the blue sky, and in the mind of man:*
> *A motion and a spirit that impels*
> *All thinking things, all objects of all thought,*
> *And rolls through all things.*
>
> Wordsworth, "Tintern Abbey"

My Favorite Poetry

It is no wonder that I (and others) savor the poetic book of Psalms. The themes of praise, creation, thanksgiving and omnipotence combine with lofty English and the inherent effectiveness of God's Word to build faith, hope and joy. Some of my favorite poets are Shakespeare, William Cowper, William Wordsworth, Whittier and the Brontës—Anne and Emily. In a future book, I will offer more suggestions for—and excerpts from—the prose and poetry of appropriate authors.

Is it moral? Is it lyrical? Is it readable? When these requirements are met, I am of the opinion that rhyming words give poetry added impact. I am attracted to anthologies, many of which are pretty as well as precious in content. The word *anthology* originates from Greek words meaning a collection of flowers.[17] One of my favorite "bouquets" is ✍ *Poems with Power to Strengthen the Soul,* compiled by James Mudge, which includes selections from various authors on themes such as faith, hope and courage. This particular book's graces are hidden within a very plain exterior. I like to read before retiring, and have filled notebooks with my selections.

✗ See authors' biographies and some of my favorite "flowers," suitable for copywork, at ***www.easyhomeschooling.com***

Poetry Tips

"Certainly no one is likely to have a taste for poetry who does not cultivate it. Yet nothing is so characteristic of the person of culture and nothing is so likely to produce true culture, as the reading and study of the best poetry."[18]

Poetry is best appreciated and understood when read aloud. An easier poet to begin with is Henry Wadsworth Longfellow. Others are John Greenleaf Whittier and Alfred Lord Tennyson. You might begin with Longfellow's "The Reaper and the Flowers," "Psalm of Life" or "The Day is Done."

A good way to begin your study of poetry is to choose one selection that you could read and reread with pleasure. Read a little about the author, then go on to read other poems by that particular poet, but only those that appeal to you. Concentrate on one author (or one book, one play or one poem) for a length of time. You may wish to read a particular poem once each day for five days. Your children could ❀ **memorize** the selection at the same time.

1) Make poetry a part of each day.

2) Start with a shorter poem.

3) Read aloud several times.

4) Do not pause at end of line, but at punctuation.

5) Memorize an entire poem or a stanza.

6) Use poetry and the Psalms for copywork and dictation.

7) Have your child write his own poem.

Mythology

"There are no fairy tales like the old Greek ones, for beauty and wisdom and truth . . . for making children love noble deeds and [for developing] trust in God to help them through."[19]

Without a knowledge of mythology, much of literature cannot be fully appreciated. Milton's short poem, "Comus," includes over thirty mythological allusions. His "On the Morning of the Nativity" contains fifteen such references. They are scattered throughout his epic, "Paradise Lost."

Various authors have attempted to provide easy-to-understand collections of the myths, such as Nathaniel Hawthorne, with his *Tanglewood Tales* and *The Wonder Book* and Charles Kingsley, author of *The Heroes.* Thomas Bullfinch hoped to give his particular work, *The Age of Fable,* "the charm of a story-book, yet by means of it to impart a knowledge of an important branch of education."[20]

> Byron, Spenser, Longfellow, Thomas Babington Macaulay and Milton are some of the authors who have used mythological characters.

Bullfinch said of his translation, "Such stories and parts of stories as are offensive to pure taste and good morals are not given."[21] He emphasized the gods and goddesses most mentioned in literature, not those ignoble portions of mythology that are rarely referred to. He hoped that his writings would be a "useful companion" in

reading, travel, conversation and in art study. He begins his fables
with this comment:

> *The creation of the world is a problem naturally fitted to*
> *excite the liveliest interest of man, its inhabitant. The*
> *ancient pagan, not having the information on the subject*
> *which we derive from the pages of Scripture, had his own*
> *way of telling the story . . . .*[22]

Mythology should be read and studied early and reviewed occasionally, particularly before a study of poetry. While some can remember
the deities and their characteristics by
reading the myths, others should commit
them to memory. This is not as daunting as it
may seem. Although there are many deities,
there are only a few facts for each that need
be remembered. (I am thankful that there is
really only one God and that he has made our
religion so simple and yet so perfect!)

> Study the
> myths before
> you study
> poetry.

To study the Greek deities, make a chart, such as a flow chart or
genealogical chart or see what **www.quickstudy.com** has to
offer. This will give you the basics of Greek mythology, but do read
the stories to add the "pictures" that are used so lavishly in literature.

> *The Greeks believed that the earth was a flat circle and that*
> *their own Mount Olympus, the abode of the gods, was the*
> *center of the world. Dividing this earth from west to east*
> *was Sea (the Mediterranean). They believed that around*
> *their circular earth flowed the peaceful River Ocean. The*
> *Greeks believed that the peoples in the northern portion of*
> *their world, the Hyperboreans, lived in eternal bliss,*
> *health, youth and springtime. The Ethiopians, in the*
> *southern part of their world, near River Ocean, were*
> *happy, virtuous and highly favored by the gods. On the*
> *western edge of their earth, was their "heaven" where*

mortals favored by the gods were transported without tasting of death. This was called Fortunate Fields or Isles of the Blessed. But, they believed, between this "heaven" and Greece were giants, monsters and enchantresses.[23]

Literature School

Even some elite colleges employ literature-based learning. Their tools are the Great Books; their principal technique, discussion. The Literature School is not only a successful school, it is the ideal multi-grade family school. Books can be read aloud together, with each child processing the information on his own level. The youngest child can narrate, the middle-aged child can write, the high schooler can report—after doing additional research about the topic, era or personality. Processing creates more lasting knowledge. I have found this easiest by requiring a written summary of the day's reading.

In narration, the child "tells back," in his own words, a chapter, a short book or a poem. This technique is a trademark of the ☞ **Charlotte Mason** method and is explained fully in her books as well as in Karen Andreola's *A Charlotte Mason Companion.* Narration is a particularly good technique to use with a younger child who does not yet write fluently. It is also effective for building English and speech skills and securing information firmly in the child's knowledge repository.

History and Literature

Histories, philosophical works, handbooks and other non-fiction works are literature only in such cases as an appeal is made to the universal emotions common to mankind. That into which no feeling can enter is not literature. History is the record of what man has done, whereas literature is the record of

> History should be learned through literature.

man's thought and emotions. The literature of a period portrays that period in the lives of the characters. Because of this, history should be learned through literature, not textbooks. Literature should have the greater emphasis because one only really knows a time by knowing the thoughts and words of the people who lived at that time.

Language Arts

When there is an emphasis on reading from a young age, language skills will be learned effortlessly. The child will write well and exhibit an expanding vocabulary in both speech and writing. You may also find, as we did, spelling class to be unnecessary.

1) Select a number of good books.
2) Set a particular time to read each book.
3) Let nothing interfere with your ❧ **scheduling**.
4) Use discussion and research to create interest.
5) Process, by writing or narrating.

✔ Each child should have the opportunity to read aloud each day. During this time you can note and correct mispronounced words.

Older Students

- Present questions that require thought. Some questions may not have one perfect answer. Some may not have an answer at all. Nevertheless, thought is stimulated and learning takes place.
- Copy challenging writing in order to practice English skills and increase comprehension.
- Do extensive research in order to understand deeper writing such as poems.
- Research authors, times and places.
- Report by presenting orally or compiling results of research in writing. The quantity and quality of written assignments should increase with older students.

• Solidify language-learning with a formal grammar course and a formal writing course such as the *Wordsmith* courses by Jane B. Cheaney.

Literature Don'ts

• *Don't* start with books with "mile-long" sentences.

• *Don't* waste your time on dumbed-down books. Although not every book worth reading will have exquisite language, be aware of poor writing and leave those books behind. After reading a few paragraphs, you will be able to tell if a particular book will foster excellence or mediocrity. See ❀ **examples of writing quality** in *Easy Homeschooling Techniques*, Chapter 3, "EasySchool Basics: How to Choose Literature," or compare the *New International Version* with the Authorized King James Bible.

• *Don't* let read-alouds fall by the wayside as workbooks, extra-curricular or other activities encroach upon your time. Schedule this time in—make it a priority. Read first unless you have babies that nap in the afternoon. In that case, afternoon may be better. But don't neglect those babies! Age three, or even younger, is the best time to began to whet your child's appetite for the nutritional literary feast of great books, which in turn will contribute to educational "health."

• *Don't* starve your family. Literature School is easy, but the menu must be rich, varied and abundant for the best results. Many books should be scheduled and many books completed. Charlotte Mason suggested so many books per day, that completion of some of them took two or more years. See suggestions for titles throughout *The Original Home Schooling Series* by Miss Mason and more tips on ❀ **literature-based learning** in *Easy Homeschooling Techniques*.

Vintage Books

Literature is only as strong as the people are strong. This is why, but
for few exceptions, the great age of literature has passed. "We deal
chiefly with the great, the enduring books, which may have been
written in an elder or latter day, but which have in them the magic of
all time."[24]

Volumes of esteemed worth are awaiting our affectionate touch
and some have been waiting long. Search the internet, attics, book-
shelves, bookstores and thrift stores. Inspect for early dates (1800s-
1940s). The condition of the book is definitely not important,
because we are seeking the gold within that we can transfer to our
childrens' hearts.

Caring for Vintage Books

Our own children were taught from an early age to handle old books
with respect. When I see someone (usually an adult) flipping pages
quickly and letting an old book flop all the way open, I cringe!
Turning pages with the finger on the inside top edge of the book,
instead of the outside edge guarantees torn pages. Opening a book
too wide or pressing it flat to copy from, cracks the hinges. It especially annoys me to see books falling over on a shelf. This will ruin a
book quickly and cause cocking. Do not
wedge the books too tightly into the bookshelf. The spine of the book should extend
beyond the shelf because it is weaker than
the boards. Pushing it back on the shelf
eventually tears the spine cloth and makes
for a shaken book.

> **Do not allow books to fall over on the shelf.**

While there are some books beyond repair and some best left to
a professional bookbinder, there are others that will not be affected
adversely by home repair. The most common repair is to put a small
bead of Elmer's Glue-All® on an inside spine edge that is pulling
away from the book. Then put rubber bands in several places around
the outside of book until the glue sets.

Both dampness and excessive dryness are enemies of books. We are talking of months or years under these conditions. It is unlikely that a short time in a dry or humid room would permanently hurt a book. In humid areas, glass cases promote mildew rather than protect. Look for inexpensive metal L-shaped bookends that have a lower section that slides beneath the books, but do slip them under the books carefully.

> Do not store books in damp basements.

Inner hinges can be strengthened by folding a narrow strip of heavy paper (index card weight) and gluing it down along the hinges, making sure it is not too long, nor too short. Torn spines can be repaired by brushing a small amount of glue on the torn portion, pressing down, and holding with a rubber band until dry. An examination will show whether the spine was designed to be loose for flexibility. If so, you will want to avoid gluing it tightly to the book. Pencil writing may be gently erased, but do not attempt to remove pen markings.

Leaving Literature

The brightest minds are those that have spent more time with words than with pictures. Television, videos, video games and computer usage occupy far too much of our precious time. How often have we done the seemingly easy thing and parked ourselves and our families in front of a TV? How many genuine family and faith-building adventures have we passed by? Have we experienced the very special bonding that takes place during the shared experience of a great book? Or, have we often thought that literature is just too difficult to tackle?

Perhaps we never managed to get past the initial difficulties and to have never discovered how interesting the best books may be . . . . We ought to wake up and take a fresh start lest we miss the finest things in life through sheer laziness . . . . For all of us life would be better worth living, would be fuller of satisfaction and more complete in accomplishment, if we could spend a certain amount of time every day with the world's best society [such as found in great books].[25]

9

Producing Fruit

*W*e enter the orchard. It is still, except for the faint droning of bees high in the blossoming trees. The air is fragrant, yet refreshing. Glittering sunlight cascades upon the leaves, and upon us. We have come to this heavenly place to learn fruit-growing techniques from the Master Gardener.

He speaks. Can it be? His voice exudes more peace than the silence! Although we know that the day will soon be over, there is no sense of hurry, for time pauses in His presence. His words pierce our innermost being with conviction, mercy, love, forgiveness and power:

> *Abide in me, and I in you. As the branch cannot bear fruit of itself, except it abide in the vine; no more can ye, except ye abide in me. . . . Herein is my Father glorified, that ye bear much fruit; so shall ye be my disciples. . . . Ye have not chosen me, but I have chosen you, and ordained you, that ye should go and bring forth fruit, and that your fruit should remain: that whatsoever ye shall ask of the Father in my name, he may give it you. . . . The fruit of the Spirit is love, joy, peace, longsuffering, gentleness, goodness, faith, meekness, temperance: against such there is no law.* (John 15:4, 8, 16; Gal. 5:22, 23)

Fruit-Growing Two Ways

- *The root of the righteous yieldeth fruit* (Prov. 12:12). We "inherited" mature apple trees when we moved into our home over twenty years ago. We planted other fruit trees, watering them well until established. Similarly, we must saturate our "root" with the water of the Word until we grow ... *unto a perfect man, unto the measure of the stature of the fulness of Christ* (Eph. 4:13). What happens if we fail to water? Self-imposed drought causes death. Fruit will never grow on such a tree.

- *Fruit trees are regularly afforded a new beginning.* So are you. Even if you feel dried-up and "dead," there is still hope with our miracle-working God. Decide to spring forth with new life.

- Strawberries and raspberries need constant weeding. Weed out sin, getting rid of what should not be there.

- *Every branch that beareth fruit, he purgeth it, that it may bring forth more fruit* (John 15:2). I learned how to prune our trees for the best yield as well as for beauty. Similarly, we should prune excesses from our lives. Prune gluttony, gossip, worry, harshness, pride and fear in order to see a fresh new growth of temperance, love, peace, gentleness, meekness and faith. Prune off unprofitable activities. Springing forth will be temperance and productivity as the Holy Spirit directs your use of time.

- Perfect blossoms develop into good fruit. A willingness to obey God is the starting place for spiritual fruit.

- Only mature trees are able to produce seed-bearing fruit. Only when we mature in Christ will our little ones grow into strong, healthy "seedlings," producing fruit of their own.

• Because fruit is usually the seed-bearing part of the plant, it is a producer, as well as a product. Our fruit produces seed for fruit in our children's lives. In addition and most importantly, spiritual fruit in abundance produces a suitable atmosphere for the Holy Spirit's presence. This is the reverse of "quenching the Spirit," whereby He is "chased away" by the works of the flesh.

☆ **Your choices dictate your life.** As parents, our choices also greatly influence our children's lives. If we consistently bear good fruit we set in motion the heritage of blessing, even unto future generations. It is urgent that we grow fruit quickly because children quickly become like their parents. If we delay fruit production or ignore it altogether, we may find ourselves with a crop of bad fruit (Prov. 1:31, Is. 3:10) such as the following. We want to painstakingly avoid this rotten or immature harvest by taking immediate steps toward growing good fruit.

• Hardness: *disrespect, emotional damage, wrath, strife.*
• Immaturity: *spiritual shallowness, etc.*
• Spoiling: *rebellion, degeneracy—sometimes unseen.*

Fruit-Growing Guide

Believers are capable of fruit-bearing because the Holy Spirit of a mighty God lives within. *According as his divine power hath given unto us all things that pertain unto life and godliness . . .* (2 Pet. 1:3). Also see Rom. 6:22 and 7:4.

Will-Training for Adults

God never forces Himself nor His ways upon us. We must choose, first, ☞ **to allow Him to come into our lives as Savior.** Next, we must choose to be filled with His Spirit (Acts 2:4; Eph. 5:18) and then we must continually choose to walk in the Spirit (Gal. 5:25)— allowing Jesus to be Lord over our daily lives, decisions and activities. We must also choose to crucify our flesh (Gal. 5:24). Simply put, this is giving up our ungodly ways and yielding to His authority. Instead of yelling, we choose to pray quietly and then speak softly. Instead of blaming, we resist the temptation to judge and find fault. There is always a way of escape if we but choose it.

If we go against what our flesh wants and instead choose the godly option, the next righteous choice will be easier. When we continually make right choices, we train our wills and develop a day-by-day, moment-by-moment relationship with the God of the universe. (John 15:4) He speaks, we listen. We obey, He blesses. This is the abiding that produces fruit and forms us into the perfect example for our children. As they see our submission to God, they submit to us, following the godly example we set.

Although the power to live this kind of life is readily available from God, the decision to choose right is not always easy. Most of us, myself included, are not there yet. It is a trick of the enemy—he does not want us walking under the Holy Spirit's control, but his. He does not want us to walk in God's blessing, but in the curse that he delights in offering us. We should want to increasingly yield to God, because the fruit is abundant and delectable! ☆ **How gratifying to know that bad was avoided, the results are perfect and blessing is ours because the decision and action was God-directed!** Contrariwise and sadly, a decision made without a sure word from God can burden us far into the future. It is imperative that we listen and obey the urging of the Spirit. I read of a man who ignored a persisting "uneasiness" he had about being in a motor-cycle race and was in a terrible accident. I have heard of others who listened and went elsewhere at the time of the 9/11 tragedy and lived to testify!

The real power for fruit-bearing is in the Bible. It is so apparent when a Christian has spent time with God, reading His words. It dramatically changes the atmosphere and the individual's nature.

•◦ Spiritual fruit begins with a consistent, intimate time with God. Spend time being quiet before Him, thinking about Him, His words and His works (creation, people, events, history, etc.). Start a notebook of special verses, prayers and answers. Look up the scriptures in this chapter (and others) and record what the Lord is telling you about fruit production. Include poems, selected verses and other appropriate excerpts. You might want to have a section in your notebook for each of the fruits.

> **Spiritual fruit grows after time in the Vine.**

➼ Deut. 30:19; Ps. 1:2, 3; Ps. 92:14; Prov. 1:29; Matt. 13:23; Mark 11:13, 14; Luke 10:27, 13:6-9; John 12:24, 14:23; Gal. 5:19-21; Eph. 4:15, 5:26; 1 John 4:19.

✔ Enforce a quiet time for your children until it becomes a firm habit. I always suggest that children keep a Bible notebook, writing daily at least a few sentences from what they read each day. Tell them to record the verses that mean the most to them and anything else they wish to include. Younger children may copy a verse or two. This notebook keeps them accountable, so that you know that they are really spending time with God. You do not need to read their notebooks. Just glance through them, to see that there is an entry for each day.

Love

Be ye therefore followers of God, as dear children; and walk in love, as Christ also hath loved us, and hath given himself for us an offering and a sacrifice to God for a sweetsmelling savour (Eph. 5:1,2).

Our God is the embodiment of all the spiritual fruits. The Word bears witness that He is so *perfectly* the characteristic of each fruit that we can say, "God is peace, God is joy, God is longsuffering," and so on.

Everything hinges upon God's love for us. He chose to suffer terribly because of His phenomenal love for us. His unconditional love, agapé, continues through the ages to say, "I will love." We must also choose to love, sometimes against great obstacles.

It is extremely challenging to love those who are not attractive or lovable, or perhaps do not treat us well or love us. The world silently says that these are not worthy of our love and to leave them to their misery. This point of view is based upon the common definition that love is a feeling of affection arising from attraction to pleasing qualities. As children of the Most High God, we are called to be different. We can love, as we choose to love. We can do all things through Christ. (Phil. 4:13)

```
God is love!
                      1 John 4:8
```

☆ **The Bible translates love as action with the right attitude.** Charity is benevolence or generosity toward others or toward humanity. While other fruits center on self, the heart of love is others. If we have the Spirit's kind of love, we will be "laying down our life" for others. This will demonstrate what God's love is like—what God is like. For example, His compassion and mercy often withhold judgment. When we have the fruit of love, we will also be slow to judge and criticize.

There is a selfish, deceitful "love" in doing for others with the motive that they will return love and favor. We are told to avoid this dissimulation (Rom. 12:9) and to hope "for nothing again." *But love ye your enemies, and do good, and lend, hoping for nothing again; and your reward shall be great, and ye shall be the children of the Highest: for he is kind unto the unthankful and to the evil* (Luke 6:35).

Provoking to Love

And let us consider one another to provoke unto love and to good works . . . (Heb. 10:24). We can provoke our children to love. Provoke means:
- To create anew, especially by means of the imagination. *The Bible and good literature provoke to love.*
- To call to mind by naming, citing or suggesting. *Remind your children of the joy they experienced when they were kind or generous to others.*

- To lead or move, as to a course of action, by influence or persuasion. *Our example (of sowing love and all the other fruits) provokes unto love. Our kind words can provoke to love.*
- To bring about or stimulate the occurrence of, cause. *God can give you creative ideas for this. It might even be by gentle force such as consequences and rewards.*

He that dwelleth in love dwelleth in God, and God in him. Herein is our love made perfect . . . (1 John 4:16,17). The more we love, serving others from our hearts as unto the Lord, the more God's love is perfected in us. Love is the essence of godliness. All of the other spiritual fruits are based upon realizing Divine love, loving God or bestowing love upon others.

➥ Matt. 25; Luke 6:35; John 15:13; Rom. 12:9; 1 Cor. 13:13; Gal. 5:13; Phil. 1:9; 1 John 3:16-18, 4:12, 19.

Joy

From childhood I was fraught with regular and sometimes deep depression. I often thought of suicide and even attempted it when in my twenties. Christ has done a mighty work in my life! Since my ☞ **new birth,** life has become more and more that proverbial "bowl of cherries." (Prov. 4:18) I am now depression-free, although the temptation is there occasionally, especially when I do not get proper sleep, when I focus on the "problems" instead of the Answer or when I step out of walking in the Spirit.

Several years ago, a dismal day loomed ahead. I was quite joyless and with "good reason." Then I began playing *Smoky Mountain Hymns, Volume II,* got out Eli's harmonica and one of our hymnals. Before long my young sons began jumping around and dancing while I rejoiced with them. What a change! We went from darkness to light, although circumstances had not changed.

Keys to Joy

- Be thankful, spotlighting the good rather than the bad.
- Know that there are wonderful surprises ahead.
- Spend time with God in the secret place of Psalm 91.
- Do what your Lord asks you to do.
- Tell others about Him and His goodness.
- Love others. (John 15:11-12)
- Share the good things God gives you.
- Keep busy. Plan and do projects.

Persecuted? Cast down? Rejoice ye in that day, and leap for joy: for, behold, your reward is great in heaven: for in the like manner did their fathers unto the prophets (Luke 6:23). It really doesn't matter what others do to us knowingly or unknowingly—Christ is on our side! (Rom. 8:31) What a great reward we have when we take persecution with a cheerful, loving attitude.

Joy is not necessarily happiness nor does it depend on outward conditions. It may be a sacrifice to be joyful when it seems there is nothing to be joyous about. Yet even in these times we can rejoice because the answer is coming and coming now! (See Ps. 16:11, Ps. 27:6, and "Faith" below.) What is depression but lack of hope? Hope and faith come through the Word of God. Jesus Himself is our joy! Joy is found in His presence. Joy is our strength. (Neh. 8:10) We cannot afford to be without it!

✗ Get busy! Each added activity, although perhaps making life more challenging, helped banish depression from my life. If necessary, force yourself to begin work on a project. Soon you will be enjoying your productivity and depression will take wing.

➻ Ps. 5:11; Hab. 3:17, 18; Zeph. 3:17; Heb. 11:6.

Peace

Thou wilt keep him in perfect peace, whose mind is stayed on thee: because he trusteth in thee (Is. 26:3). If we keep our thoughts on the promises of God, which reveal the Prince of Peace, we will learn we can trust Him. This will give us "perfect peace." How do we keep our minds stayed on Him? Throughout the day, take prayer breaks. Meditate on Scripture.

One definition for peace is *freedom from quarrels and disagreement.* There is a path to peace and harmony. First of all, we need to be full of the Spirit and have personal peace, as above. Next, we have to obey the Spirit's still small voice. Do we need to stop what we are doing to pray with one or two of our children? Do we need to be more of a servant to our husbands? Have we failed to form necessary habits? Sowing the right actions will result in the fruit of peace. *Let us therefore follow after the things which make for peace, and things wherewith one may edify another* (Rom. 14:19).

> He is our Peace—if we let Him be.

"To keep the peace" means to maintain or observe law and order. One of the most helpful ways to have peace in the home is to ❀ **maintain order.** When one has no schedule, no system of accountability, there is the least peace. When we have order, peace and happiness increase. Daily schedules must be set and enforced.

We can have peace in the midst of a storm. We will not be afraid of evil tidings if our hearts and minds are fixed on God. We then realize that we are held tightly with love and that our Father will take care of everything!

✔ Look up "peace" with your children in a *Nave's Topical Bible* or a concordance. Studying God's Word will change the atmosphere. Study and ❀ **memorize** passages about peace.

✗ Write particularly helpful scriptures on index cards. You can also do this with a verse you are memorizing. Carry the cards with you or tape them up throughout your home. (Deut. 11:20)

•◦ Ps. 119:165; Prov. 3:1, 2; 1 Cor. 14:33; Eph. 2:14; Phil. 4:9; 2; Thess. 3:16; James 3:18; 1 Pet. 3:10; 2 Pet. 1:2, 3:13, 14.

Longsuffering or Patience

The Lord . . . is longsuffering to us-ward, not willing that any should perish, but that all should come to repentance (2 Pet. 3:9). God's highest purpose and heart's desire is that all be saved. This is why He is longsuffering. While some of us want judgment to fall—and fall immediately!—on the sin centers of this world and on those who have wronged us or our loved ones, God says, "Just a little longer, and perhaps they will open their lives to me."

Longsuffering is akin to forbearance. (Rom. 2:4; Eph. 4:2) To forbear means *to be tolerant or patient in the face of provocation.* We are to be merciful enough, kind enough, humble enough and meek enough to forbear or "put up with" a person, place or thing and walk in forgiveness.

Perhaps you are in the "hothouse" of longsuffering. These perfect conditions are ideal for growing what seems to be a bitter fruit. I know how difficult it is to thank God for situations that are really bad! However, we are told do just that. *In every thing give thanks: for this is the will of God in Christ Jesus concerning you* (1 Thess. 5:18). True thanksgiving acknowledges that God sees things we do not see about the situation. Longsuffering is more palatable when we yield ourselves to the Father's supernatural wisdom.

Thanking Him does not mean we have to go on forever with things as they are. There is always the assurance of sweet deliverance. He will bring victory as we stand in longsuffering, faith and the other spiritual fruit. However, in most cases, we must go against our inclination to try to "fix" things. Our acts or words usually hinder the result we desire. Instead we should focus on what God would have us to do, letting Him be the fixer.

Patience, another word for longsuffering, means *to bear or endure pain, difficulty, provocation or annoyance with calmness.* It implies that we are calmly awaiting the outcome or result without being hasty or impulsive. When we are walking in longsuffering we are resting in the LORD—waiting for and expecting Him to act. (Ps. 37:7) The Christian who comprehends the power of the Word, because he or she has meditated on it regularly, will still be standing—patiently enduring wrongs or difficulties—when others have fallen. God wants the world to see that He never fails the one who has faith in Him. Our longsuffering encourages others to repentance, righteousness and eternal life.

Hold on! Your change is coming soon. The promises He makes, He keeps. Stand on His promises. Never give up, never give in and it won't be long. You can make it! *And so, after he had patiently endured, he obtained the promise* (Heb. 6:15). Put on the following! (Col. 3:12, 13)

- Bowels of mercies.
- Kindness.
- Humbleness of mind.
- Meekness.
- Longsuffering.
- Forbearing one another.
- Forgiving one another.

✗ Turn from the evil of a situation by filling your mind with the pure and lovely. Put more and more of the living Word into your heart. Our view of the Word of God must get in line with the actuality. It is esteemed more than the name(s) of God and is even equated with God in the Scriptures. (See Rev. 19:13, Ps. 138:2 and the book of John). When you get in this frame of mind, your view of the situation will change and you will become the conqueror that God has created you to be.

➤ Job 23:10; Ps. 86:15; Prov. 25:15; Jer. 15:15; Zech. 13:9; Rom. 9:14; 2 Cor. 6:7; Eph. 4:1, 2; Col. 3:13; James 5:8; 1 Pet. 1:7.

Gentleness

Gentleness comes forth effortlessly from oneness with the Holy Spirit as fruit emerges from a tree. Do we have to go out and shake a tree so that it will produce fruit? Do we have to talk to or cry over that tree? No! All we have to do is let it happen. Similarly, as we continually cling closely to Christ, gentleness will be available when we need it most. Gentleness is a matter of the heart. Does our heart move with compassion when we hear of a total stranger or even fictionalized character losing a loved one or being hurt in some way? If the fruit of gentleness is abundant in our hearts, even a portrayal in a book or movie will sadden us. Are we gentle with the least of his creatures? Disregard for—or cruelty to—animals is the opposite of this fruit. Females seem to have more natural gentleness. Most of us would rather talk to the animals than hunt them! God made us this way because we are the child-bearers and gentleness is crucial for nurturing children. Perhaps we need to stir up this gentleness. When we are filled with the loving Presence of God, we will neither offend Him nor the little lambs He has entrusted us with. Meditating on how gentle He has been with us will cultivate our gentleness with others. *He shall feed his flock like a shepherd: he shall gather the lambs with his arm, and carry them in his bosom, and shall gently lead those that are with young* (Is. 40:11).

Gentleness Checklist

❑ Considerate? *Concerned about the needs and feelings of others?*

❑ Kindly in disposition? *Sympathetic, helpful, agreeable, pleasant?*

❑ Amiable? *Friendly in disposition, good-natured, likable?*

❑ Tender? *Protective, loving, given to sympathy or sentimentality?*

❑ Mild and soft? *Avoiding harshness and severity?*

❑ Merciful? *Compassionate, kind and forgiving?*

Over forty times in the Bible we are told that the Lord's mercy endures forever! Does ours? Are we critical of others behind their backs? *Speak evil of no man, . . . be no brawlers, but gentle* (Titus 3:2). Are we sometimes short-tempered and unmannerly? *The servant of the Lord must not strive; but be gentle unto all men, apt to teach, patient* (2 Tim. 2:24).

Gentleness is not weakness but power. *He teacheth my hands to war; so that a bow of steel is broken by mine arms. Thou hast also given me the shield of thy salvation: and thy gentleness hath made me great* (2 Sam. 22:35, 36). Gentleness can "break the bone"—can break bad. *By long forbearing is a prince persuaded, and a soft tongue breaketh the bone* (Prov. 25:15). *A soft answer turneth away wrath: but grievous words stir up anger* (Prov. 15:1).

> **Gentleness is crucial for nurturing children.**

Gentleness is related to our natural disposition. This word, disposition, is defined as one's usual mood, a habitual inclination or tendency. We can have a supernatural disposition as we allow the Holy Spirit to fill us with His fruit of gentleness.

➥ 2 Samuel 22; Ps. 86:15, 103:8, 145:8, 9; 2 Cor. 10:1; Eph. 4:32; 1 Thess. 2:7, 8; Heb. 3:13; James 5:11.

Goodness

Genuine goodness is rare in this perverse world. Many Christians have been so tainted by current-day culture that they do not even recognize sin. My strongly-held opinion is that we need a "good washing" and a total separation from worldly ways. (Eph. 5:26, 2 Cor. 6:17) *Be not conformed to this world: but be ye transformed by the renewing of your mind, that ye may prove what is that good, and acceptable, and perfect, will of God* (Rom. 12:2).

Goodness is marked by virtuous character and actions. The word *virtue* is defined as *moral excellence and righteousness.*

Virtue, especially in medieval times, was considered primarily a manly characteristic. Who can find a virtuous man in these times? Even some Christians seek perverse "pleasures" behind closed doors, while the most "manly" pagan would be quite amused if asked whether he had reached this pinnacle of manhood. We should thank God often for our godly men!

Goodness can mean chastity, courage or valor. A turn-of-the-century *Webster's Dictionary* declares that goodness is *moral rightness or righteousness, marked by actions which are just and in conformity to moral law or divine precepts.* Therefore, the best examples of goodness are found from Genesis to Revelation. God is love, and His unending goodness began when He created a perfect world with all its systems. *He loveth righteousness and judgment: the earth is full of the goodness of the LORD* (Ps. 33:5).

There are two sides to this fruit—being good and doing good. They are inseparable. *A good man out of the good treasure of his heart bringeth forth that which is good* (Luke 6:45). Doing good exhibits itself in selflessness—caring enough about others to give them our time.

> Goodness is defined as beneficence— *the state or quality of being kind, charitable, or beneficial.*

Charity was a lifestyle in the past. Christian women were charitable first at home, then to those of God's family, then to neighbors, but never neglecting strangers. We are to be good to all. *He that doeth good is of God* (3 John 1:11). *But love ye your enemies, and do good, and lend, hoping for nothing again; and your reward shall be great, and ye shall be the children of the Highest: for he is kind unto the unthankful and to the evil* (Luke 6:35). *Be not overcome of evil, but overcome evil with good* (Rom. 12:21).

Being good results from living in union with Christ and following the Good Shepherd in word and deed. *But it is good for me to draw near to God* (Ps. 73:28). *For he satisfieth the longing soul, and filleth the hungry soul with goodness* (Ps. 107:9).

➥ 2 Ex. 34:6; Ps. 65:4; John 5:29; Rom. 2:4; Eph. 5:9; 1 Tim. 6:17.

Faith

Faith is my favorite fruit and for good reason. *But without faith it is impossible to please him: for he that cometh to God must believe that he is, and that he is a rewarder of them that diligently seek him* (Heb. 11:6). The best place to be in faith is walking in the goodness of God, using faith to resist the devil as in Psalm 91. I believe the "secret place" mentioned therein is the place of faith. Faith is complete trust in God and will multiply all the other fruit.

> *Blessed is the man that trusteth in the LORD, and whose hope the LORD is, for he shall be as a tree planted by the waters, and that spreadeth out her roots by the river, and shall not see when heat cometh, but her leaf shall be green; and shall not be careful in the year of drought, neither shall cease from yielding fruit* (Jer. 17:7, 8).

Faith produces optimism because faith says the best is yet to come. *Faith is the substance of things hoped for, the evidence of things not seen* (Heb. 11:1). *What He had promised he was also able to perform* (Rom. 4:21).

Faith Basics

- God is the doer, and the glory is exclusively His. *That your faith should not stand in the wisdom of men, but in the power of God* (1 Cor. 2:5). No attribute of ours, no strength or natural gift, could do what God can do. Seeing the answer come through faith alone gives God the most glory—and gives us the most joy.

- Faith comes by hearing the word of God. Faith is the result of the realization that God is big enough. We become acquainted with this *God Who is More Than Enough* through His words, found in the Bible.

- Faith is built by prayer. *But ye, beloved, building up yourselves on your most holy faith, praying in the Holy Ghost* (Jude 1:20).

- Faith is not sight. This is the hard part—to believe without seeing. But we will see! First with our spiritual eyes and then with our physical eyes. God has promised and *God is not a man that he should lie* (Num. 23:19). Our part is to get, stay and stand in faith.

- Faith is not a dirty word! The faithless are the ones who displease God. *And Jesus answering said, O faithless and perverse generation, how long shall I be with you, and suffer you . . .* (Luke 9:41)? *Now the just shall live by faith: but if any man draw back, my soul shall have no pleasure in him* (Heb. 10:38). In Mark 4:40, Jesus expresses his astonishment at the faithless when He says: *How is it that ye have no faith?* Yes, it is astonishing that we have no faith when we say that we know the Miracle Worker!

- Faith not only pleases God—faith works wonders. (Acts 3:16, 6:8) Time will not permit me to tell of all the wonders He has done in my own life through faith alone. I have walked in health for many, many years and plan to continue based on Deut. 33:25 (*. . . as my days, so shall my strength be*). How can this be possible, when the world is running to doctors? I resist each slight temptation toward sickness immediately, knowing Jesus has already paid the price and it stops immediately (1 Pet. 2:24, Deut. 28:61 with Gal 3:13). I believe and say, "Devil you are a liar! I am redeemed from the curse of the law." Since no plague comes nigh me (Ps. 91) I need not go nigh a health facility. I have also included my children in my "faith prayers" and they have also been spared untold medical visits and costs.

More Benefits of Faith

- Access to God (Eph. 3:12)
- Protection (Eph. 6:16, Ps. 91)
- Victory (1 John 5:4)

•➤ Search the Scriptures for other benefits of faith.

✗ To grow "faith fruit," meditate on the Word of God, especially those scriptures telling who God is, what He has done and is doing. He is Creator and Sustainer of everything. Sometimes we see through a glass darkly about what (in the world!) He is doing in our lives, but it is perfectly obvious to see God in nature. Consider His Resurrection power! Think of the Red Sea miracle and the other Exodus miracles. Recall the miracles in your own life that you may have forgotten about.

Add to your Faith

- Standing (James 1:6, 7)
- Doing (James 2:17)
- Hoping (Ps. 62:5, 1 Pet. 1:21)
- Speaking (Mark 11:23)
- Loving (Gal. 5:6,1 Cor. 13:13)

Loving makes faith living and effective. *And because iniquity shall abound, the love of many shall wax cold* (Matt. 24:12). It's tough to love today, but we must stay in love if we want to see full results of our faith. We must stay in faith if we want to please God.

We must choose to put complete faith in the One who desires to show Himself strong on our behalf. Sometimes all other options become exhausted because God wants this compete trust from His children. Many do not believe they should resist a bad situation, but rather accept it as God's will. Some do not even realize the deceitfulness of the devil in their situation. How easily he sometimes steals, kills and destroys! God does not want His children's eyes to be blinded to the devil's dirty tricks. We cannot help someone who refuses to activate their faith and "fight the good fight" but we need to be strong in faith for those who are too weak to believe God for themselves. Then we will not hesitate to pray for the sick, expecting them to be healed; we will not fear in the face of urgent needs, nor will we worry.

➥ Ex. 15; 2 Chr. 16:9; Ps. 91; Jer. 32:17; John 10:10; Rom. 4:20, 8:32, 10:16; 2 Cor. 5:7; 1 Tim. 6:12; 1 Pet. 1:21, 5:8.

Meekness

A shocking letter full of accusations and lies arrived and I stepped totally out of meekness. I should have recognized the source (Rev. 12:10; John 8:44) immediately and combated spiritually. Instead, I angrily set things straight! It was a release, true, but after my emotional reaction, I was sobbing spiritually because I had taken a giant step backwards from the solution for *faith . . . worketh by love* (Gal. 5:5).

Walk in the Spirit, and ye shall not fulfil the lust of the flesh (Gal. 5:16). The Lord had wanted to prepare me by my morning Scripture reading, telling me He was my defense, my defender. (Ps. 62:6) A wiser course would have been praying and waiting. That was my way of escape. (1 Cor. 10:13)

How do we overcome our remorse? Even Peter wept bitterly for having failed Jesus. If we fall, restoration follows our godly sorrow. We can make amends. Rom. 12:21 says, *Be not overcome of evil, but overcome evil with good.* The Lord dropped a gift into my lap at that moment and I sent it on to the one who had offended me, with apologies.

To be meek is to be mild, soft, unassuming and humble. These qualities grow from a root of unselfishness. We are told to seek meekness, follow after it and put it on. (Zeph. 2:3, 1 Tim. 6:11; Col. 3:12) *Take my yoke upon you [put it on], and learn of me; for I am meek and lowly in heart: and ye shall find rest unto your souls* (Matt. 11:29). Our Divine Example—the One True Creator God, worthy of the highest homage—is meek and lowly in heart! Taking His yoke upon us results in peace and rest for our souls.

The Lord highly esteems children. (Matt. 18:2-5) We should never chastise or discipline with an assumed and carnal air of authority. *Brethren, if a man be overtaken in a fault, ye which are spiritual, restore such an one in the spirit of meekness* (Gal. 6:1). In all our correcting, we should be meek in admitting our common weaknesses, along with emphasizing the supernatural provision for victory.

Views on Meekness

The meek are not those who are ne'er at all angry, for such are insensible, but those who, feeling anger, control it, and are angry only when they ought to be. Meekness excludes revenge, irritability, morbid sensitiveness, but not self-defence or a quiet and steady maintenance of right.

Webster's Encyclopedic Unabridged Dictionary

Meekness is a form of love. If a man smite you in the face, your bodily nature says: "Smite him back again." If a man betrays you in the bitterest way, nature, in the bad sense of that term says: "Give him as good as he sent." What is meekness? It is receiving personal injury, yet having such a predominant spirit of love in you that you wish the man that does it good. It is not retaliation, it is being so filled with the love and nature of Jesus Christ that you give back blessing for railing and cursing, prayers for those that despitefully use you.[1]

Henry Ward Beecher

Humility is strong, not bold; quiet, not speechless; sure, not arrogant.

Estelle Smith

Writings on Meekness

- "The Lamb" by William Blake
- "The Wind and the Sun" by Aesop
- "The Gentlemen" by John Henry

➥ Num. 12:3; Ps. 22:26, 25:9, 37:11, 45:4, 147:6; Is. 29:19; Zeph. 2:3; Eph. 4:1-3; Phil. 2:3; 2 Tim. 2:25; Heb. 11:26.

Temperance

Know ye not that they which run in a race run all, but one receiveth the prize? So run, that ye may obtain. And every man that striveth for the mastery is temperate in all things. Now they do it to obtain a corruptible crown; but we an incorruptible. I therefore so run, not as uncertainly; so fight I, not as one that beateth the air: But I keep under my body, and bring it into subjection: lest that by any means, when I have preached to others, I myself should be a castaway (1 Cor. 9:24-27).

Temperance—*egkrateia*—means mastery or self-control. *Webster's 1828 Dictionary* defines it in detail as moderation and patience:
1) Moderation—*particularly habitual moderation in regard to the indulgence of the natural appetites and passions; restrained or moderate indulgence such as temperance in eating and drinking or temperance in the indulgence of joy or mirth. Temperance in eating and drinking is opposed to gluttony and drunkenness and in other indulgences, to excess.*
2) Patience—*calmness; sedateness; moderation of passion.* To temper means *to soften; to mollify; to assuage; to soothe; to calm; to reduce any violence or excess.*

We should strive for mastery in every area of our life. Even excess mirth is looked upon as madness! Do we have an argumentative bent? This needs to be tempered with love. Do we have an intemperate mouth? We need to work at keeping our lips sealed. Do we spend more time than we should at the computer, on some hobby or other pastime? This must be tempered and overcome with God's priorities for His glory, and our good. How about food? We need be temperate both in the amount of food we eat, as well as the kinds of things we put in our body. What about emotions? Emotions can indicate immaturity, lack of faith or a negative attitude often displayed as negative, harmful words.

➡ Make a list of areas in your life that need "tempering." Star or circle the most important ones and begin immediately to do what you must to produce this desirable fruit in your life.

> We should stive for mastery in every area of our life.

Being filled with the fruits of righteousness, which are by Jesus Christ, unto the glory and praise of God (Phil. 1:11). Being filled with temperance and every other spiritual fruit not only brings glory to God but delivers unimaginable blessings to our doorstep. Stepping into the flesh hinders the delivery.

The Sun Sets

Our time together has come to a close. As the setting sun sinks beneath the horizon the sky is flushed with the most breathtaking hues we have ever seen. The Holy Spirit leads us out of the orchard just as the birds begin their twilight lullabies. We have had a full day.

New Birth Diary

Excerpts from the Most Important Year of my Life
Maui, Hawaii

December 25, 1975

Lorraine, may your New Year be the most fulfilling year of your life so far. May you find yourself, thereby find true happiness.

January 1, 1976

Happy New Year, Girl. One day at a time, you'll make it through this year. With God's help it will be a better one. You can be a better person.

January 6, 1976

I'm in a rut
I feel routine, maybe I need
A change of scene.

Who am I? Who am I really? What will it take to make me happy?

> *Do you know where you're going to?*
> *Do you like the things that life is showing you?*
> *Where are you going to?*
> *Do you know?*
> *Do you get what you're hoping for? . . .*
> *What are you hoping for?*
> *Do you know?*[1]

January 20, 1976

I don't know where I'm going, but God does. He has a plan for me.

May 23, 1976

Met "Bully" in a bar. He talked about Jesus, and later showed me scripture after scripture in a little booklet. There was an earthquake and I was afraid, but he said, "If you really believe in Jesus, you don't have to be afraid of anything." In my mind, I saw Jesus on the cross and was immediately saved and freed from fear and the desire to sin.

May 25, 1976

The past has passed away forever! Praise God! I was born again. I found myself. This is what I waited for, for so long. Thank you, Lord. I have finally accepted You into my heart and it is filled to overflowing with gratitude and Your love.

August 5, 1976

Loving You is all I really need. My life is so complete—completed in Yours. My heart is your home. You waited with open arms for so long.

I was sleeping
But now I see . . .

You're everything—
Everything to me.

> *I love you in a place where there's no space or time. I love you for my life. You are a friend of mine. You taught me precious secrets of the truth—withholding nothing. You came out in front and I was hiding. But now I'm so much better—now we're alone and I'm singing this song to You.*[2]

August 8, 1976

"The Lord and I, We got so close, He filled me with the Holy Ghost."

August 29, 1976

Baptized in the Pacific Ocean. Living waters surged around me!

October 24, 1976

Oh Lord Jesus, my **Sweet, Sweet Comforter.** I love You and give You all the praise for bringing me this far, for increasing my faith, day by day, through Your Holy Word, worship and fellowship. Thank You for bringing me through this year, for answering my searching cry by your gift of salvation and truth. Help me to be more and more like You. Guide me into Thy perfect will. Keep me humble—destroy my pride. I love You, Jesus, and I want You forever in my life.

November 11, 1976

My heart explodes with thanksgiving and love for You, **Perfect Unselfish One.**

December 25, 1976

The year, 1977, will be the best year of my life because when you know the Lord it just gets better and better. Merry Christmas, Lorraine—and thank You, Jesus, for making this Christmas—my first Christmas with You—so perfect, so special, so real—because You live.

May 23, 2003
It's a Good Life

It has been over twenty years since Jesus came into my life. I have never regretted that decision and never will. I have had untold blessings since that day. Particularly, His deep love took heart-pain and loneliness from me. In addition, He set me in a family and blessed me with children.

Do you really know God? Have you met Him? Has there been a recognizable change in your life? If not, all else in this life is worthless. What's more, you have no chance for heaven—yet.

However, the **One Who Loves You** is not wanting you to live in agony in hell forever and has made a way. Let Him replace your strivings with His perfect and wonderful plan. *And ye shall know the truth, and the truth shall make you free* (John 8:32). All you need to do is say yes in your heart. You don't have to have a vision or go to a church. You don't have to clean up your life first. If you are sincere, He will meet you wherever you are.

For supernatural power to live the Christian life, to share the Good News with others and to walk an anointed life (where all you do and say is especially effective), say yes to all that Jesus has for you and be filled with the Holy Spirit. Then you be able to "pray without ceasing" (Rom. 8:26 Acts 2:4) which will build you up in the most holy faith.

If there are vibrant God-praising, Word-preaching churches where you live, get involved, especially in attending services. I need not emphasize the importance of Scripture—I already have through-out this book. Contemplative reading of God's Word is even more important for the new Christian.

Lorraine Curry

Top 10 Book List

See reviews of some of these titles in Chapter 7, "Reaping from Reviews."

1

Easy Homeschooling Techniques
Lorraine Curry

True, this book was influenced by some of the books on this list, but as I reviewed many other books, it was evident to me that there was a need for an easy-to-follow, succinct guidebook.

2

Marva Collins' Way
Marva Collins and Civia Tamarkin

With great literature and love Marva turned ghetto children around to self-respect and a love of learning. You can do the same! One of the earliest books that I read, along with John Holt's *How Children Learn* and *How Children Fail.*

3

You Can Teach Your Child Successfully
Ruth Beechick

This is a very practical book. Skip the chapter on math and use flash cards and *Saxon.*

4

The Successful Homeschool Family Handbook
Dr. Raymond and Dorothy Moore

The Moore formula of education balances study, work and service, and is garnished with a healthful lifestyle. It reinforces the home-schooling choice and helps one be a gentler, more resourceful and efficient parent-teacher.

5

Original Homeschooling Series
Charlotte Mason

Pure Charlotte Mason. A wealth of information. Many words and many ideas. Study with a highlighter—as I did—to mine the kernels of gold.

6

A Charlotte Mason Companion
Karen Andreola

A Charlotte Mason Companion provides an abundance of information on—and examples of—the Charlotte Mason method. Karen includes chapters on Shakespeare, Dickens, poetry, composition, picture study, grammar, vocabulary, spelling, history and Mother Culture (a term trademarked by the Andreolas, meaning activities that enrich the mother). Included are three chapters on narration and more than three on nature study.

7

Charlotte Mason Study Guide
Penny Gardner

Pure Charlotte Mason—in small servings. Want quick inspiration? Read a few quotes! Penny has gleaned the best of Miss Mason in this slim but powerful volume. To Miss Mason's words, Penny adds a sprinkling of her own suggestions making this a good value, especially if you would rather not undertake the *Original Homeschooling Series.*

8

A Charlotte Mason Education
Catherine Levinson

Great little introduction to the Charlotte Mason method.

9

A Survivor's Guide to Homeschooling
Luanne Shackelford & Susan White

Good basic content in this book that was first published when modern homeschooling was in its infancy.

10

For the Childrens' Sake
Susan Schaeffer MacCauley

Exhortation to be gentle with your children. Should be read at least once a year!

Resources

2. Pursuing Better Parenting

No Greater Joy Ministries
1000 Pearl Road
Pleasantville TN 37033
www.nogreaterjoy.org

3. Cultivating Christian Curriculum

Home School Treasures
450 Golden Nuggett Way
Maysville GA 30558-3802
706-652-2258
hstreasures@juno.com
www.hstreasures.com

Vision Forum
4719 Blanco Road
San Antonio TX 78212
Orders: 800-440-0022
210-340-8525
Fax: 210-340-8577
info@visionforum.com
www.visionforum.com

Tobin's Lab, Inc.
Mike Duby
15055 Glen Verdant Drive
PO Box 725
Culpeper VA 22701
540-937-7173
mike@tobinslab.com
www.tobinslab.com

4. Drawing from my Diary

The Lester Family
PO Box 203
Joshua Tree CA 92252
760-366-1023
info@lesterfamilymusic.com
www.lesterfamilymusic.com

Mantle Ministries
228 Still Ridge
Bulverde TX 78163-1878
830-438-3777
Fax: 830-438-3370
steve@mantleministries.com
www.mantleministries.com

Vision Forum
See Chapter 3, above.

Kids Art
PO Box 274
Mt Shasta CA 96067
530-926-5076
Fax: 530-926-5076
info@kidsart.com
www.kidsart.com

Second Harvest Curriculum
43668 355th Ave.
Humphrey NE 68642
Orders: 877-923-1682
www.usedhomeschoolbooks.com

Contenders for the Faith
Keepers of the Faith
404 S Mine St
Bessemer MI 49911
906-663-6881
Fax: 906-663-6885
sales@keepersofthefaith.com
www.keepersofthefaith.com

Home School Treasures
See Chapter 3, above.

Simply Spelling
Shoelace Books
3086 Juhan Road
Stone Mountain GA 30039
www.shoelacebooks.com

7. Reaping from Reviews

Language Arts . . . the Easy Way
Rushton Family Ministries
1225 Christy Lane
Tuscumbia AL 35674
256-381-2529
time4tea@hiwaay.net
www.cindyrushton.com

The Real Life Homeschool Mom
Virginia Knowles
1925 Blossom Lane
Maitland FL 32751
homenews@juno.com
www.thehopechest.net

Home School, High School, and Beyond...
Castlemoyle Books
The Hotel Revere Building
PO Box 520
Pomeroy WA 99347-0520
509-843-5009
Fax: 509-843-3183
johnr@castlemoyle.com
www.castlemoyle.com

God and Government
Vision Forum
See Chapter 3, above.

8. Loving Literature

Exceptional Books
God's Gardener
PO Box 95
Boelus NE 68820
308-996-4497
Fax: 308-996-9104
Orders: 866-263-5959
info@easyhomeschooling.net
www.easyhomeschooling.com

The Charlotte Mason Research & Supply Company
PO Box 758
Union ME 04862
www.charlottemason.com

$\mathcal{E}$ndnotes

Preface

1   Christopher Schlect, *A Critique of Modern Youth Ministry* (Moscow ID: Canon Press, 1995) p. 4.
2   Eve Curie, *Madame Curie* (New York: The Literary Guild of America, 1937) p. 49. *Manya was Marie's nickname; author, Eve, her daughter.*

1. Gathering Flowers

1   Christine Sorensen, personal correspondence, April, 1981. *Christine planted the day lilies in 1917. The Sorensens lived in our house from 1917-1961.*
2   Mary Hale Woolsey, "Springtime in the Rockies," 1926.
3   Edwin H. Morris, "When Your Hair Has Turned to Silver," 1930.
4   "Farewell" was written to the old Irish air "Moll Roone." *Thomas Moore was not only very financially successful because of his ballads but was considered to be an equal to Byron, Shelley and Scott. His work was translated into many languages, thus popularizing Irish music throughout the world.*
5   James Flannery, *Dear Harp of My Country* (J. S. Sanders & Co., 1997).
6   "Polish Americans," *Cobblestone History Magazine for Young People,* 7 School Street, Petersborough, NH 03458 (Cobblestone Publishing, 5/1/95).
7   *Rockville Centennial Book* (Cairo, NE: Record Printing, 1986) p. 24.
8   Jane Healy, Ph.D., *Endangered Minds* (New York: Touchstone. 1999).
9   Presentation Statement by the translators to King James, found in some editions of the King James Bible.
10 Mary Pride, *Practical Homeschooling* (Home Life, Inc., 1997).

11 Helena G. Street, *Our Books, Our Wings* (Lincoln, NE: Nebraska Library Commission, 1989) p. 200.

12 *Beautiful Girlhood* (Eugene, OR: Great Expectations Book Co.).

13 Article based on information from "Psychiatry, Education's Ruin." *Includes facts on Ritalin, an addictive and controlled substance. Some "ADD" children go on using street Ritalin in their teens, and some have suffered withdrawal symptoms as severe as suicide. This free booklet can be requested by calling 800-869-2247.* **www.cchr.org**

14 Gail Riplinger, *New Age Bible Versions* (A. V. Publishing, 1993).

15 Benjamin Bloom, *A Taxonomy of Educational Objectives* (United Kingdom: Longman Group, 1969). *Bloom also said the end result of education "was personal values/opinions with no real right or wrong answers."* (as quoted in Ron Sunseri's *Outcome-Based Education—The Truth about Educational Reform* [Oregon: Questar Publishers, Inc., 1994] p. 14.)

16 Derek Prince, *Blessing or Curse* (Chosen Books Publishing Co., 1990).

2. Pursuing Better Parenting

1 Thomas W. Handford, *Beecher: Christian Philosopher, Pulpit Orator, Patriot and Philanthropist* (Chicago: Donohue, Henneberry & Co., 1887) p. 119.

2 Roosas John Rushdooney, *The Philosophy of the Christian Curriculum* (Vallecito, CA: Ross House Books, 1981) p. 123.

3 Tedd Tripp, *Shepherding a Child's Heart* (Wapwallopen: Shepherd Press, 1995) p. 16.

4 *Webster's New International Dictionary of the English Language* (Springfield, Mass: G. & C. Merriam Company, 1913).

5 Tripp, p. 61.

6 W.A. Welch A.M., *How to Study, A Guide for Pupils' Self Improvement in School and Home* (Chicago: W.M. Welch & Company, 1889).

7 Tripp, p. 37.

8 Welch, *How to Study.*

9 Ibid.

3. Cultivating Christian Curriculum

1 Rousas John Rushdoony, *The Philosophy of the Christian Curriculum,* (Vallecito: Ross House, 1985) p. 61.

2 J. O. Engleman, *Moral Education in School and Home* (Chicago: Sanborn & Co., 1918).

3   Engleman.
4   "New Media" (Tacoma: *The News Tribune,* 2001) August 6, 2001.
5   Why Learn a Foreign Language: "Why Learn Spanish?" **www.open.org/~coflt/why_learn_fl.htm#spanish** (May 10, 2003).
6   **www.homeschool.com/articles/nobel/bio** (May 10, 2003).
7   Engleman.
8   United States Department of Education (1995).
9   *McGraw—Hill Parent Newsletter,* Tracy Dills, editor, March/April 2002, Vol. 4, Issue 2.

5. Harvesting from History

Antiquarian books provided primary source material for this chapter.

1   John Gill, *Systems of Education* (Boston: D.C. Heath 1886) p. 15, 16.
2   Gill, p. 18.
3   Gill, p. 24.
4   John Locke, "Some Thoughts Concerning Education." The History of Education and Childhood. **www.socsci.kun.nl/ped/whp/histeduc/locke/index.html** (July 5, 2002).
5   E. L. Kemp A.M., *History of Education* (Philadelphia: Lippencott, 1909) p. 257, 258.
6   Kemp, p. 260.
7   John Gill, *Systems of Education* (Boston: D.C. Heath, 1886) p. 43.
8   Gill, p. 45.
9   Gill, p. 49.
10 Gill, p. 57, 58.
11 Gill, p. 57.
12 Gill, p. 51-53.
13 Gill, p. 50.
14 Gill, p. 61.
15 Levi Seeley Ph. D., *History of Education* (New York: American Book Co., 1904) p. 258.
16 Aimee Natal, "The Life and Times of Charlotte Mason, Part II." Mason Series, 1998. **mnatal.members.easyspace.com/masonseries2.htm** (July 5, 2003).
17 William H. Kilpatrick, "Introduction to Johann Heinrich Pestalozzi." *The Education of Man—Aphorisms* , The Home of Informal Education. **www.infed.org/thinkers/et—pest.htm** (July 5, 2002). *See also:*

J. H. Pestalozzi, *How Gertrude Teaches her Children* (1894).

K. Silver, *Pestalozzi: The Man and His Work* (London: Rutledge 1965).

18 John Gill, *Systems of Education* (Boston: D.C. Heath 1886) p. 104.

19 University of London Library. **www.aim25.ac.uk/cgi—bin/search2?coll_id=2154&inst_id=14** (July 6, 2002). *Emanuel Swedenborg said, "All people who live good lives, no matter what their religion, have a place in heaven."* The Swedenborg Church in North America. **www.swedenborg.org** (July 6, 2002).

20 Gill, p. 76.

21 Seeley, p. 283.

22 Seeley, p. 274.

23 Seeley, p. 277.

24 Seeley, p. 275.

25 Seeley, p. 287.

26 Spartacus Educational. **www.spartacus.schoolnet.co.uk/USAdewey.htm** (July 6, 2002).

27 John Dewey, as quoted in Minerva. **www.ul.ie/~philos/vol1/dewey.html** (July 6, 2002).

28 Frank M. Flanagan. "John Dewey" 1994. Minerva. **www.ul.ie/~philos/vol1/dewey.html** (July 6, 2002).

29 Spartacus Educational. **www.spartacus.schoolnet.co.uk/USAdewey.htm** (July 6, 2002).

30 Spartacus, **www.spartacus.schoolnet.co.uk/USAlafollette.htm** (July 6, 2002).

6. Raising the Standard

The Recitation by Samuel Hamilton, Ph.D., cited below, provided primary source material for this chapter. Both direct excerpts and edited paraphrases were used.

1 W.T. Harris Ph.D, LL.D., *Webster's New International Dictionary of the English Language* (Springfield: G. & C. Merriam Co.,1912) p. 1782.

2 Samuel Hamilton, Ph. D., *The Recitation,* Lippincott Educational Series, Vol. 5 (Philadelphia: Lippincott and Co., 1906) p. 25.

3 Hamilton, p. 30, 31.

4 Hamilton, p. 24.

5 Hamilton, p. 68.

6 Hamilton, p. 357.

7 Hamilton, p. 77.

8 "Memory and Related Learning Principles." Intelegen, Inc. 2000. **web—us.com/memory/memory_and_related_learning_prin.htm** (July 10, 2002).

9 Katti Gray, "The Hard Road to Learning." Long Island: Our Story. **www.lihistory.com/5/hs504a.htm** (July 15, 2003).

10 Hugh King, director of education for the Town House Museum, an East Hampton facility that initially doubled as a meeting place and as one of Long Island's first one-room schools, as quoted by Katti Gray, "The Hard Road to Learning." Long Island: Our Story. **www.lihistory.com/5/hs504a.htm** (July 15, 2002).

11 "History of Lanesfield School" Johnson County Museums (KS). **kcsun4.kcstar.com/schools/JohnsonCountyMuseums/ lfhst.htm** (July 16, 2002).

12 " Schoolmaster Jacob Strickler at Hirzel (1791—1853)" Strickler Stories. **www.strickler.dolphins.ch/stor-e.htm#1791— 1853** (July 16, 2002).

13 Ibid.

7. Reaping from Reviews

1 Charles Kingsley, *The Heroes—Greek Fairy Tales for my Children.*

8. Loving Literature

1 Charles W. Eliot, Ph.D., "The Delphian Movement," *The Delphian Course,* Vol. 1 (Chicago: The Delphian Society, 1922) p. x.

2 Jane M. Healy, *Endangered Minds: Why Our Children Don't Think* (New York: Simon & Schuster, 1990).

3 William J. Long, *Outlines of English and American Literature* (Boston: Ginn and Company, 1917) p. 4.

4 Eliot.

5 Long, p. 5.

6 Long.

7 Long, p. v.

8 Brander Matthews, *Introduction to American Literature* (New York: American Book Company, 1896) p. 9, 10.

9 Rueben Post Halleck, *History of English Literature* (New York: American Book Company, 1900) p. 130.

10 Halleck, p. 250.

11 Halleck, p. 333.

12 Stanley J. Kunitz & Howard Haycraft, *British Authors of the Nineteenth Century* (New York: H.W. Wilson Company, 1936) p. 21.

13 Long, p. 248.

14 W.A. Welch A.M., *How to Study . . .* (Chicago: W.M. Welch & Company, 1889) p. 37.

15   Halleck, p. 186.
16   Sherwin Cody, *How to Read and What to Read* (Rochester: Sherwin Cody School of English, 1944) p. 25.
17   W.T. Harris Ph.D, LL.D., *Webster's New International Dictionary of the English Language* (Springfield: G. & C. Merriam Co., 1912) p. 95.
18   Cody, p. 49.
19   Karen Andreola, *A Charlotte Mason Companion* (The Charlotte Mason Research and Supply Co., 1998) p. 211.
20   Thomas Bullfinch, *The Age of Fable,* The World's Great Classics (New York: Grolier) p. 5.
21   Bullfinch, p. 6.
22   Bullfinch, p. 22.
23   Bullfinch, p. 8-11.
24   Eliot.
25   Cody, p. 8, 10.

9. Producing Spriritual Fruit

1   Henry Ward Beecher, as quoted in James B. Pond, *A Summer in England with Henry Ward Beecher* (New York: Fords, Howard, & Hulbert, 1887).

New Birth Diary

1   Gerry Goffin and Michael Masser, Theme from *Mahogany* (Screen Gems, EMI Music Inc. and Jobete Music Co. Inc., 1973).
2   Adapted from *A Song for You* by The Carpenters.

Index

$\mathcal{H}$

$\mathcal{I}$

$\mathcal{J}$

K

$\mathcal{L}$

T

U

V

Businesses of Interest
Classified and Display Advertising

Usborne Books at Home
Deb Blencowe
Independent Usborne Consultant
Richardson TX
888-353-5496
972-690-9919
UBsales@blenco.com
www.blenco.com

Do you love books? Want to earn FREE books OR earn commission, travel and bonuses? Over 1000 titles for all ages. Ask about offer EHC2002.

Audio Memory
501 Cliff Drive
Newport Beach CA 92663
800-365-SING
www.audiomemory.com

Sing along and learn Grammar, World Geography, States & Capitals, Math, U.S. History, Bible, Science and more!

Joy of Learning
Customer Service: 800-490-4430
707-964-7040
learn@joyoflearning.com
www.joyoflearning.com

Discount homeschool supplies for preschool through high school including Bob Jones, Alpha Omega and Sing Spell Read & Write.

Professor Phonics

4700 Hubble Road
Cincinnati OH 45247
Toll Free: 866-385-0200
Fax: 513-385-7920
Sue@professorphonics.com
www.professorphonics.com

Award winning intensive phonics curriculum. Age 4 and up. Reads in 3-6 months! Begins reading in first lesson. Self-teaching interactive CD rom.

Atelier Homeschool Art

4615 Rancho Reposo
Del Mar CA 92014
858-481-4223
Toll free: 888-760-ARTS
Fax: 858-481-3959
arts@homeschoolart.com
www.homeschoolart.com

The *Atelier* art program was comprehensively tested to ensure outstanding results. Using video-based teaching methods, *Atelier* provides the homeschooler with unprecedented ease of use, breadth of scope, and results-oriented validation.

Gazelle Publications

11560 Red Bud Trail
Berrien Springs MI 49103
800-650-5076
info@gazellepublications.com
www.gazellepublications.com

Products to help ordinary parents become excellent teachers. Find several chapters plus discounts on line. Help for families in financial hardship.

CENTRIFUGE LANGUAGE ARTS

3611 C.R. 100
Hesperus CO 81326
800-900-1907
eva@centricurriculum.com
www.centricurriculum.com

Complete comprehensive coverage of all six areas of language. Superior curriculum gives the best results. K-12.

Getty-Dubay Italic Handwriting Series

Portland State University
Extended Studies
Continuing Education Press
866-647-7377
8am-5pm M-F PST
press@pdx.edu
www.cep.pdx.edu

The Getty-Dubay Italic Handwriting Series for children and adults is preferred by homeschoolers, legible because it's loop-free, and effective because it makes sense. Call or email for a free brochure and desk strip.